Handwritten notes:
1. Carbeth
2. Balmaha
3. Inverarnan
4. Bridge of Orchy
5. Kinlochleven

THE
WEST
HIGHLAND
WAY

W9-BII-221

Official Guide

TENTH EDITION

*Revised and updated by
Roger Smith from an original text
by Bob Aitken*

THE WEST HIGHLAND WAY

BIRLINN

First published in 1980 by HMSO
Second, third and fourth editions published by HMSO
Fifth, sixth, seventh and eighth editions published by
    Mercat Press
Ninth edition published by Birlinn Ltd

This tenth edition published in 2013 by Birlinn Ltd
West Newington House
10 Newington Road
Edinburgh
EH9 1QS

Reprinted 2015

ISBN: 978-1-78027-115-6

Printed in China through World Print Ltd

CONTENTS

ACKNOWLEDGEMENTS

THE development of long distance routes in Scotland has not been without controversy, but as the routes have matured they have catered for an ever-growing number of walkers, bringing enjoyment to many and economic benefits to rural communities. As the first long-distance route in Scotland, the West Highland Way has served as a flagship for the network, and it remains the most popular, catering for an estimated 80,000 walkers (in full or in part) each year. Scottish Natural Heritage (SNH) remain indebted to all those who assisted in its development, including proprietors and their agents, estate workers and Forestry Commission staff, local authority officials and local people along the route. Since being officially opened in 1980, the Way has been well served by its countryside rangers and by its managing authority, the West Highland Way Management Group on behalf of Argyll & Bute Council, East Dunbartonshire Council, Highland Council, the Loch Lomond and The Trossachs National Park, Stirling Council and Scottish Natural Heritage.

The first edition of this guide, published in 1980, was compiled and written by Robert Aitken, who in addition to undertaking the exhaustive background research which has led to the guide's informative and often amusing historical and anecdotal evidence, also spent many days walking the route. It is to his credit that so little of his original text has had to be amended in preparing this and the previous revised editions; changes have largely been confined to factual matters where the line of the Way has been altered or where village services have expanded in response to the number of users. Every effort has been made to make the information as up-to-date and practical as possible, but changes will inevitably occur between editions.

In the period in which the Way has been in existence, the managing authorities and SNH (and its predecessor body, the Countryside Commission for Scotland) have gained much useful information and opinion from those who have used the route. Surveys have been undertaken to gauge the level of use, expenditure patterns and, most importantly, users' enjoyment of the route and how they consider it could be improved.

The many letters received with praise or criticism of the Way have also been appreciated, and we take this opportunity to invite readers to comment on the route or on this guide. Only through your comments will the managing authorities be able, with support, to improve the management and services along the Way. Please write to:

West Highland Way Development Officer,
West Highland Way Management Group,
Loch Lomond and The Trossachs National Park,
20 Carrochan Road,
Balloch G83 8EG.

Or you can email to: *whwmailbox@lochlomond-trossachs.org*.

The publishers' thanks are due to the WHW Development Officer for his help in checking the text and mapping, and to the following for use of photographs: the West Highland Way Management Group, Lorne Gill of SNH, Alan Forbes, Charles Gulland, Roger Smith and Erl Wilkie.

ALONG THE WAY

This section deals with the practicalities of your journey along the West Highland Way, and gives general advice to supplement the route description in the main part of the guide. Much of this material will be familiar to outdoor enthusiasts in general and to experienced long-distance walkers in particular, but others may have less idea of what to expect on the Way and how to prepare for it. It is worth saying that while many sections of the West Highland Way are straightforward going on excellent, well-drained paths and tracks, some parts are much rougher and will make for slower progress. There are stretches which, by British standards, are remote not just from human habitation but from any form of shelter; and the Way is liable to get more than its fair share of wet and windy weather, even in summer. Those tackling the whole route must realistically expect to have at least some wet going both overhead and underfoot.

Please note that the West Highland Way is primarily a long distance *footpath*, and although some sections are suitable for mountain bikes and horse riders, others are not designed to withstand repeated use by these groups.

Direction and season

If you wish to tackle the Way as a complete trip, we strongly recommend that you travel south to north, from Milngavie to Fort William; the guide has been written with this assumption in mind. At the simplest level – and this also applies to those tackling shorter sections of the Way – as you head northwards you will have the sun at your back, rather than in your eyes, and are more likely to have wind and rain behind you, or on your left flank, than in your face. The stages between accommodation and supply points are longer, and there is more uphill work, on the northern part of the Way, so that the southern start offers a gentler 'warm-up'. Above all, however, the northwards journey has a greater aesthetic appeal, in its progression from the urban through the domestic and pastoral to the wild mountain and moorland country, and in the scenic crescendo of the last quarter north of Kingshouse, where the switchback from ridgecrest to valley creates a vivid sense of mountain travel. The opposite progression from north to south has its own attractions, but inevitably lacks that positive climax.

When should you walk the Way? Although July and August are normally the warmest time of the year, they are not necessarily the driest. There is much to recommend May and June, tradition-ally the months of lowest rainfall in Western Scotland and often blessed with settled periods of warm dry weather, with diamond-sharp visibility and 18 hours or more of daylight. These months, with April, are also among the best for the naturalist, since spring flowers are in bloom and birds are nesting, while the tree canopy is still relatively open and does not inhibit bird-watching as it can do later. The bracken which in autumn can tower over head-height on open slopes is still low and freshly green, and midges are less of a nuisance. In the mountain country, there may well still be a lingering wreath of snow on the tops to sharpen the line of ridge and corrie.

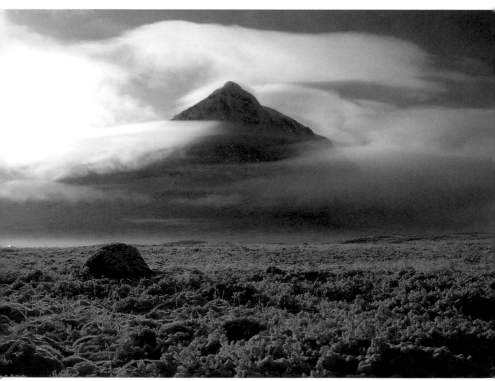

Buachaille Etive Mor in winter.

The long-established Scottish Six-Day Motorcycle Trials are held in the first week of May each year. This event often uses sections of the Way between Bridge of Orchy and Fort William, and the latter town, as the event headquarters, is very busy with bikes, riders, support teams and followers. The event is a remarkable spectacle, but those wishing to avoid the disturbance of the bikes can get advice from the Ranger Service in Glen Nevis (westhighlandway@ highland.gov.uk) or from the route website, *www.west-highland-way. co.uk*. The event itself has a website at *www.ssdt.org.uk*.

July and August are the high tourist season in the Highlands generally, and there will be heavy corresponding pressure on accommodation. Hotels may be fully booked and bed and breakfast places are often taken up fairly early in the day, particularly in bad weather, when you might be most inclined to look for a roof over your head. While such potential difficulties can be avoided by booking ahead, they do reduce your freedom to change plans in response to weather or personal inclination. Starting your walk midweek rather than the weekend will make finding accommodation easier. As most people start the Way on a Saturday or Sunday, many accommodation places are busy for one or two nights a week but much less so the rest of the time. Starting midweek will also provide a quieter and 'wilder' experience.

Accommodation difficulties lessen during the autumn, which has the added splendour of changing colours in farmland, woodland and moorland: late September and October will usually see the finest effects. Undeniably there is a higher risk of wet and windy conditions, but the first frosts can bring glowing days of unblemished clarity and rich colour. Winter can be grim or glorious, sodden wet or snow-blanketed, gale-swept or frost-bound; and again accommodation can become a challenge as some hotels, hostels and bed and breakfast places are closed.

Following the Way

The West Highland Way has been comprehensively but unobtrusively marked on the ground by the managing authorities, using standard signposts and waymark posts to the Scottish Natural Heritage specification. All the waymarkers can readily be identified by their dark brown colour-stain and by the SNH long-distance

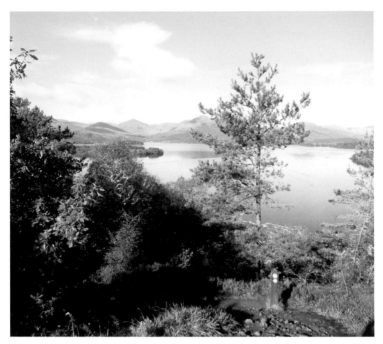

West Highland Way marker near Loch Lomond.

footpath symbol, a thistle within a hexagon. Signposts and way-mark posts with yellow arrows are found where the Way changes course. Confirmation markers bearing the symbol alone show the line of the Way where, for example, it passes a junction of paths without turning, or where it crosses open fields or moorland without any other directional aids, such as a fence or a dyke, to follow.

The general policy is to keep the number of waymarkers to a minimum consistent with safe route-finding. Thus there are fewer markers on sections where the line of the route is already clear, as on forest roads or along the shore of Loch Lomond. The Way is marked in detail on Ordnance Survey maps and on the special 1:40,000 map sheet prepared by Harveys to accompany this guide, and reference to the map should clear up any difficulties.

The longitudinal 'shape' of the West Highland Way presented an awkward problem of mapping, which has been cleverly resolved by the use of a long strip of map divided into sections. This avoids the need to insert a large number of map pages in the guide, or to purchase five standard OS 1:50,000 Landranger sheets (64,

57, 56, 50 and 41) or seven 1:25,000 Explorer maps (342, 347, 348, 364, 377, 384 and 392). The special map obviously covers a limited corridor of country, and should be supplemented by the appropriate Landranger or Explorer sheet if you are moving off the line of the Way, to climb a particular hill, for example.

Times and distances

The guide avoids any detailed suggestion of timing for the route. Every party will be different in composition and fitness, in interests and inclinations, and in the weight of the packs its members carry. Weather, underfoot conditions and length of daylight are extra variables to be considered. There is nothing worse than to feel constrained, however subconsciously, by someone else's idea of how long it should take to cover a given distance.

Most walkers should be able to complete the Way in a week; this gives an average of about 21 km (13 miles) a day – and a user survey showed that the normal time taken was, in fact, six or seven days. Some can do it much faster; on the other hand it would be perfectly possible to spend a fortnight or more along the West Highland Way, particularly if you take the opportunity to explore the country around it, and to climb some of the grand hills that overlook it.

Much of the Way gives easy going in good conditions, on well-established footpaths, forest roads, historic military roads, and former railway lines. On these sections, walkers can make a rough estimate of the time required for the distance by using Naismith's Rule, named after its originator, a founder of the Scottish Mountaineering Club, and a prodigious walker himself. The rule allows one hour for every 5 km (3 miles) on the flat, with an additional half-hour for each 300m (1000 feet) of climbing. Extra allowance should be made for heavy packs or poor conditions.

This guide divides the Way into eight sections accessible by public road at either end. If you are tackling the route in short stretches, you should find that these sections break the Way up into convenient stages; if you are backpacking, you will make your own stages in response to weather conditions and your needs for accommodation and services.

Accommodation

Given that the West Highland Way passes through a good deal of sparsely-populated country, there is an adequate supply of accessible accommodation along its length, but not so much that it can be taken for granted. As already mentioned, in the high season there is pressure on all forms of accommodation, while in winter some of it closes down.

Detailed information, including phone numbers, is provided in the West Highland Way Pocket Companion prepared annually by the West Highland Way Management Group (WHWMG), and available from them, from local tourist information centres or as a download from the Way website. You should always check accommodation details in advance, as local circumstances can change quite rapidly. Contact details for VisitScotland and tourist information centres along the Way are given at the end of this section.

The 'Walkers/Cyclist Welcome' Schemes

The WHWMG and VisitScotland promote a scheme whereby accommodation establishments can, if they wish, display a 'Walkers Welcome' or 'Cyclists Welcome' symbol in their windows (you may also see Dog or Horse Friendly signs and indications of WiFi availability). These indicate that the proprietors are willing to cater for the particular needs of these groups, and should ensure a warm welcome. In return, Way users are asked to consider the needs of the proprietors and of other guests.

Please bear in mind that many establishments along the Way cater for visitors whose needs differ from walkers/cyclists. Not everyone will readily tolerate the problems caused by bulky, wet packs and muddy boots! The Walkers/Cyclist Welcome schemes should mean that courteous walkers and cyclists get a courteous welcome.

Hotels and Guest Houses

Hotel accommodation is available at regular intervals, but many of the hotels are small, or cater for a specialised clientele such as fishermen; so it is sensible – especially in summer – to book in advance if possible. The Way's *Pocket Companion* and website have all the necessary details for hotels on the route, or you can contact VisitScotland on 0845 2255 121 or *www.visitscotland.com*.

Bed and Breakfast is offered in a fair number of places along the Way, especially in the villages. However, there is little accommodation of this type between Rowardennan and Crianlarich, simply because the country is so thinly populated. The Crianlarich-Tyndrum area and Kinlochleven are well provided, but a long way apart. Much of the B&B trade is casual, so walkers must compete with other visitors, but you can book ahead using the information in the *Pocket Companion*. You can keep your schedule flexible by telephoning in the morning to reserve accommodation for that evening. It may also be possible to hire a static caravan for a night on one of the caravan sites by the Way, particularly outside the peak season. Some accommodation providers will provide a pick-up and drop-off service which can also enable you to unpack for a couple of days and travel light.

It is worth noting here that mobile phone coverage of the area cannot be guaranteed, due to the nature of the terrain, and therefore should not be relied on as the sole means of communication.

Hostels

The Scottish Youth Hostels Association has three hostels on the Way. Rowardennan is open March-October; Crianlarich is open March-October and winter weekends; and Glen Nevis is open all year. These are available only to members of Youth Hostel associations, but it is possible to join the SYHA at any of the hostels. At all three it is advisable to book accommodation for Easter, July and August, and other holiday weekends. Full details of membership, and the current leaflet, can be obtained by contacting the national office: SYHA, 7 Glebe Crescent, Stirling FK8 2JA (*www. syha.org.uk*).

Bunkhouses and Private Hostels

Bunkhouses offer a similar range of facilities to those provided in youth hostels, at equivalent prices. In many cases these form part of a larger facility, such as an hotel or restaurant, offering additional services including meals and refreshments. Space can be limited, so it is advisable to book in advance at peak periods. There are bunkhouses at Balmaha, Rowardennan, Inversnaid, Tyndrum, Kingshouse, Kinlochleven, Fort William and Glen Nevis. There is also a bunkhouse at the Bridge of Orchy Hotel, although at present there are no self-catering facilities. Bar meals are available in the hotel.

Some of these bunkhouses are part of the growing network of private hostels in Scotland. For a full list of these hostels, go to *www.hostel-scotland.co.uk.*

Wigwams

A number of 'wigwam' shelters have been provided along the Way. These intriguing wooden structures offer simple accommodation in the form of a sleeping platform but no other facilities. Most are sited on farms, and at other places you may come across similar things called 'hobbit houses' or 'tepees'. There are also 'microlodges' (wooden shelters sleeping 4 people) at the Glencoe Mountain Resort. The wigwams, which sleep up to 6 people, can be pre-booked, and a modest charge is made for their use. You will find them at Easter Druimquhassle Farm near Drymen; Beinglas Farm, Glen Falloch; and Auchtertyre Farm in Strath Fillan. For details see the Way *Pocket Companion* or the website.

A 'wigwam' along the route.

Camping

Without doubt camping is the most free and flexible mode of accommodation for anyone on a long-distance route; it liberates you from the ties of pre-booked lodgings, and lets you go or stay as weather or fancy dictate. On the other hand, camping implies gear and hence a much heavier pack: the West Highland Way calls for a waterproof tent with flysheet and a good sleeping bag. Camping also brings more intimate contact with the natural environment, and a greater responsibility to care for it.

Many people tackling the whole of the Way will be backpacking, using one of the many excellent lightweight tents available. Use recognised campsites where these are available (they are listed in the *Pocket Companion*). Try to avoid camping in the vicinity of houses, in or near forestry plantations, anywhere livestock is grazing, or on grouse moors.

The recent Scottish access legislation includes a right to camp wild for one or two nights, but this right must be exercised responsibly. Attitudes to campers will be determined by their behaviour: courtesy, tidiness and consideration for others are important. Under no circumstances should open fires be lit, and always be absolutely scrupulous about toileting and taking every piece of litter away with you for proper disposal.

Sanitary arrangements are especially important. If you need a latrine, dig a hole well away from your campsite and a good distance from any watercourse to avoid the risk of pollution. Cover the waste matter and burn any toilet paper used. A useful leaflet, *Where to 'Go' in the Great Outdoors*, is available free from the Mountaineering Council of Scotland, as is an advice leaflet on wild camping (*www.mountaineering-scotland.org.uk*).

Please note that camping restrictions apply from 1 March to 31 October in the National Park between Drymen and Inverarnan. Further details from *www.lochlomond-trossachs.org* or the Way website.

Services and supplies

The route description in the guide gives a general outline of the service facilities and shops available on and near the Way. Note that there is no centre with a population of over 2,000 between

Milngavie and Fort William, and that there are only small villages between Drymen and Kinlochleven. Don't expect shops in these places to hold large or specialised stocks: plan your supplies in advance.

Managing the Way

A heavily-used route such as the West Highland Way demands a considerable management effort to keep it at the quality demanded by its users, and some notes on the current management regime operating along the Way may be of interest.

The Way is managed by a number of organisations that are represented on the West Highland Way Management Group. These are East Dunbartonshire Council, Stirling Council, Argyll and Bute Council, The Highland Council, and Loch Lomond and The Trossachs National Park Authority. Additional funding to support the businesses and communities along the route is provided by European LEADER+ programmes. Ranger services are provided by East Dunbartonshire Council (based at Mugdock Country Park), Stirling Council (based in Stirling), Loch Lomond & The Trossachs National Park (based at Balmaha) and Highland Regional Council (based in Glen Nevis). There are also National Trust for Scotland rangers at Ben Lomond and in Glencoe, Blackmount Estate has a ranger and the RSPB at Inversnaid has a Reserve Warden.

While on the route you may also see maintenance teams. They try to keep abreast of any work required, but they and the rangers are always grateful for reports of damage to route infrastructure, etc. Please be specific if you make such a report – it is frustrating to be told that 'there's a stile broken near Tyndrum' as this could cover a substantial area. The revenue cost for maintenance is currently (2013) nearly £400,000 per year. This covers replacement of worn-out, broken or damaged items such as stiles, gates and footbridges; interpretive signs; waymarks and finger-posts; and Way 'furniture' generally.

It is fair to say that the going for walkers has improved considerably over the past 30 years. By using this guidebook you are helping; a percentage of the proceeds from sales is used as a contribution towards the maintenance of the route.

Charity Events and Races

A popular route such as the West Highland Way is bound to attract organised events, and it is possible, especially in summer, that you might encounter participants in one of these.

The largest current annual event is the Caledonian Challenge, which takes place in June. It involves teams walking or running 54 miles of the route (Fort William to Auchtertyre Farm in Strath Fillan) and raises substantial sums for designated charities. The event usually attracts over 1,000 participants plus support teams, marshals, etc. For more details go to *www.caledonianchallenge.com*. There is an annual West Highland Way race, also held in June. The current record time for the complete Way is an astonishing 15½ hours.

Transport

Since the West Highland Way follows a relatively low-level route through hill country, it tends to parallel the main lines of road and rail communication and is rarely far from them. As a result it is quite possible, with a little planning, to complete the Way in short sections using public transport to return to a base or to the starting point. The guide is divided into a series of such sections, ending at points accessible by public road; at the start of each section an outline is given of the means of transport available.

As far as Balmaha the Way is never more than a short distance from a bus route; from Inverarnan northwards it runs roughly parallel with the West Highland Railway to Bridge of Orchy, and with the A82 road to Kingshouse Hotel at the head of Glencoe. On Loch Lomond during the summer, WaterBus services provide cross-links to the west shore, and from Tarbet to Inversnaid, calling at Luss and Rowardennan (see the *Pocket Companion* for more details). There is also an 'on demand' ferry between Ardleish and Ardlui.

Naturally, since much of the country of the Way is sparsely populated, most of the train and bus services are not frequent, even in summer: three or four services per day is about normal. Timetables change from year to year and you should check the current position by contacting Traveline on 0871 200 22 33 (7am–10pm every day) or visiting *www.travelinescotland.com*, The

WaterBus services at Tarbet.

transport terminals in Glasgow and Fort William or any of the Tourist Information Centres along the route will also have travel information.

Weather

The West Highland Way runs in and over mountain country on the west side of Scotland, so almost by definition it is subject to very changeable weather at any time of year, and particularly to windy and wet conditions. In general terms, rainfall increases as the Way goes north and as it climbs to higher altitudes. Thus, while the average annual rainfall in the Glasgow area is around 1,000 mm (40 inches), and is not a great deal higher at the southern end of Loch Lomond, by the head of the loch it has risen to twice that figure. The mountains west of Rannoch Moor, in Glen Coe, and above Kinlochleven have rainfall levels approaching that recorded on Ben Nevis, well over 3,000 mm (100 inches). By way of consolation the valleys are slightly drier; Kinlochleven and Fort William each record around 2,000 mm (80 inches). West Highland rainfall has what the meteorologists call 'a low coefficient of variation' which means it is unlikely to be much more or less than the average in any given year.

As a rule, about five-eighths of this precipitation falls during the winter half of the year, so a good deal of it is in the form of snow. In a normal year snow covers the summit of Ben Nevis for all but 75 days, and lingers into May on many of the mountains near the Way. Below 300 metres (1,000 feet) snow is unlikely to lie for more than 30 days in total.

This reflects the relative mildness of the weather on the whole. Summer average temperatures are not high – the typical July figure is around 13º-15ºC (the upper 50s F) – and these fall quite quickly with altitude, but winter averages and extremes are less cold than further east towards the centre of Scotland. January average temperatures near sea level will usually be 3º-4ºC (up to 6º-8ºF) above freezing. The trend appears to be for these temperatures to increase slightly, but also for more extremes of wet and windy weather.

Wind is the real enemy, particularly in combination with rain or snow. South-westerlies predominate. Wind-speed rises markedly with altitude: Glasgow gets about six days with gales a year, Ben Nevis about 50. The higher stretches of the Way tend to be bare and open and are thus exposed to the full force of the wind. Wind and rain together in these circumstances make for a risk of exposure, and you should know and watch for the symptoms in all members of the party.

Gales can strike at any time of the year. As far as other weather conditions are concerned, early summer has already been recommended. In a normal year, April, May and June will be the driest months in the country around the Way, usually getting less than 20% of the annual rainfall between them. August can be very wet; at Fort William on average almost twice as much rain falls in August as in May. As a corollary of this, May is generally the sunniest month of the year, enjoying about a sixth of the year's total hours of bright sunshine. Nevertheless, it is usually 4º-5ºC (about 8ºF) cooler than the warmest month, July.

Particularly at higher levels along the Way the weather can change with startling speed from good to bad or vice versa. This should be borne in mind when pitching camp, or when setting off on one of the upland sections of the route. In doubtful conditions it may be helpful (if you can) to listen to BBC Radio Scotland (92–95 FM or 810 medium wave) for a local forecast, or call at a Tourist Information Centre or ranger base, where weather forecasts are often displayed.

The managing authorities have tried to take account of all weather conditions in preparing the Way, particularly in providing footbridges on burns, but in extreme weather even a tiny burn can become a fearsome torrent. Such exceptional conditions rarely last long and it is generally wiser to retreat and wait out foul weather in shelter rather than risk a soaking or even a drowning. On the other hand it is not a good idea to wait for mist to clear from high ground. Cloud can cling to the hills for days on end. A party that lacks the ability to find its way in mist should not venture on the upland stretches of the West Highland Way.

Equipment

The West Highland Way is essentially a long hill-walking/cycling expedition, and unless you plan only to tackle a short distance over the more straightforward sections south of Drymen, you should equip yourself as for the hill.

Starting from the ground, a pair of walking boots, with moulded rubber soles, are basic items. Trainers or walking shoes invite wet feet and would be a liability on the rougher parts of the route; wellington boots are certainly quite appropriate on some sections, but would be risky on others, and are rarely comfortable over any long distance. Anklets or gaiters are useful over boots at any time of year to keep out water, snow or mud.

Trousers (not jeans) are very much a matter for personal preference; shorts can be carried as an option but it would be folly to wear them as the only form of leg covering. Waterproof trousers are essential. The usual 'top' of a light, warm shirt and fleece – with a spare in the rucksack – should be augmented by one or more outer layers, the combination of which is both windproof and waterproof. Gloves or mitts, and a balaclava or woolly hat, should be carried at all seasons. The phrase 'it can be winter any day of the year on the Scottish hills' may be hackneyed, but it is true.

Equipment should also include the usual safeguards and route-finding aids – map, compass, torch and whistle; some emergency food; and a small first-aid kit: even one or two roller bandages can be invaluable in case of an accident. Midge repellent is recommended between June and mid-October. Plastic bags are useful. A big one can double as an inner waterproof lining for the rucksack and an emergency bivvy bag, while smaller ones can keep individual items like spare clothing and food dry and separate from one another. They are invaluable for campers, not least in keeping order in a cluttered tent. In winter or early spring you may need an ice-axe (and of course know how to use it) if you want to climb any of the mountains around the route.

If you wish to camp, your load will be a good deal heavier and a comfortable well-packed rucksack is of prime importance. Since nights can be chilly even in summer, a good quality sleeping bag is a great comfort; and you must carry your own stove.

Training and Preparation

Particularly if you are unaccustomed to rough walking or off-road cycling, or to carrying a substantial pack, it will pay dividends in enjoyment to do some preparatory training for the Way. Every opportunity should be taken to work up the muscles; new gear – especially boots or pack – should be well broken in; and the equipment to be carried should be ruthlessly reviewed to cut down on weight.

From the experiences of users surveyed on the Way, a few practical points of advice may be useful:

- carry the absolute minimum of gear commensurate with being adequately equipped. You should never carry more than a third of your own weight, and for comfort 10 kgs (22 lbs) would be a desirable target weight;

- don't rush at the Way, especially if you are not fully fit. If you overdo it on the first day, it may take most of the rest of the Way to recover;

- attend to blisters, ankle chafing and other foot problems as soon as you become aware of them;

- if in doubt about the line of the Way, sit down and work it out from map and guide, rather than pushing on hopefully and possibly in the wrong direction.

Pests

At any time between May and October, insect pests can be a nuisance. In the earlier part of the season, clegs (horse-flies) can give a nasty bite; later on, sheep-ticks may be a problem – you should avoid sitting in deep grass or bracken, particularly if you are wearing shorts.

Clegs and ticks seem to have good and bad years, but midges are never in short supply. Clouds of these tiny stinging insects can make camping, or even stopping for a few minutes, a purgatorial experience, especially in July and August. They are most active in calm, warm and humid conditions; fortunately even a light breeze will keep them down. It is well worth bearing this in mind when selecting a campsite.

If you are walking the Way in high summer, you may well find that a good insect repellent is worth its weight in gold. Repellent 'candles', for burning inside a tent, are also available as are midge-coils for burning outside. It is best – though far from easy – to abstain from scratching midge-bites, as they subside quickly; but if you are sensitive to insect bites, you should carry an appropriate lotion to treat them.

Going on the Hills

One of the particular attractions of the West Highland Way is that it passes close to many striking and attractive hills. You may well be keen to tackle a few of these, and the guide outlines some suggestions for ways up the most obvious peaks. However, bad weather can strike suddenly to turn even the simplest climb, on paths like those on Ben Lomond or Ben Nevis, into a serious and potentially dangerous expedition. Although there are straightforward routes on most of the hills around the Way, many of them are bounded by steep, broken corries or crags; and to go astray on the ridges can bring a party down into remote and pathless country on the wrong side of the hill.

You should, therefore, prepare for any climbs that appeal to you by having a good look at the appropriate OS Landranger or Explorer map sheet, and by consulting guide books. The series of regional guides produced by the Scottish Mountaineering Club can be recommended, but there are plenty of other excellent sources. The wider background knowledge gained in this way brings an extra enjoyment to days on the hill. You should also consider whether your proposed climb might interfere with deer-stalking or lambing (see the later sections in this chapter).

Access in Scotland

The Land Reform Act came into full effect in February 2005. The Act gives the public a general right of access to all open countryside in Scotland, with the provision that this access must be exercised responsibly. There are exceptions to the general right such as in the vicinity of houses or other buildings, on industrial sites, airports and railway lines, and military areas. Access rights can be temporarily suspended for estate management activities such as shooting deer or grouse, at certain times of the year.

The rights also include a right to camp wild for one or two nights, again provided you do this responsibly and keep away from houses or other buildings. The rights and responsibilities of the public and of land managers are explained in the Scottish Outdoor Access Code which can be found at: *www.outdooraccess-scotland.com*.

Simplified versions of the Code are available in leaflet form (*Know the Code before you Go*) at Tourist Information Centres or from Scottish Natural Heritage (*www.snh.gov.uk*). The principal points emphasised in the Code are as follows:

- Take personal responsibility for your own actions, and act safely.
- Respect people's privacy and peace of mind.
- Help land managers and others to work safely and effectively.
- Care for your environment and take your litter home.
- Keep your dog under proper control.
- Take extra care if you are organising an event or running a business.

Safety on the Hills

When you are in hill country you should follow the Mountain Code:

- Think carefully before you go alone.
- Leave written word of your route with someone responsible and report your progress at the first opportunity.
- Plan within your capabilities.
- Know the local weather forecast.
- Watch the weather and amend your plans accordingly.
- Be properly equipped.
- Know how to use map and compass.
- Know the mountain distress signal – six regular whistles/flashes a minute, repeated at one-minute intervals.
- Know simple first-aid and the symptoms of exposure and hypothermia.
- Eat little and often to maintain energy.
- Keep alert all day.

In the event of accident or emergency, dial 999 and ask for the Police. Mobile phone reception is variable across the West Highlands and can depend on which network you are using. Signals are often better higher up; in the valleys there can be 'black spots' where reception is poor or non-existent.

Lambing and Calving

Walkers are asked to take particular care during the lambing season, which stretches from February on low ground farms to May on the hill farms. If ewes or lambs are encountered during this period, do your best to avoid disturbing them. Pregnant ewes can panic if taken by surprise, and can lose their lambs, which is a financial loss to the farmer. Please don't pick up 'lost' lambs: they're not. Go round rather than through flocks of sheep at all times. Stand still if sheep show signs of nervousness. Do not under any circumstances take dogs anywhere near them.

Cattle will also be encountered along the Way, and the same care should be taken with them. They tend to be curious and may advance rather than retreat. Don't panic and run unless an animal

A blackface lamb.

is obviously aggressive. Cows and bullocks will frequently run up, stop and take a good look at you. A stick can be useful in shooing them away. Avoid exciting them or you will make matters worse. In the event of meeting a bull, ram or other animal that you are unsure of, go round it if possible with an eye to escape routes, or retreat and seek another path.

Cows are extremely protective of young calves and particular care should be taken at this time. Dogs should not be taken into fields with cattle, particularly if calves are present. If you do have a dog with you and a cow or bull shows signs of aggression, it is better to let the dog go and ensure your own safety.

Deer-stalking

The Scottish Highlands hold a large red deer population, representing not only a superb feature of local wildlife but a valuable economic resource. Since they have no natural predators, the adult deer must be culled to maintain a healthy population and to reduce their impact on agricultural land. Thus the sport of deer-stalking is at once a recreation, a valuable form of tourism, and an ecological necessity. It provides employment and helps to conserve the rural environment.

Stag stalking is largely carried out between mid-August and late October. Hillgoers can cause direct disturbance to deer which makes the stalking more difficult. During this critical period, you should consider how you can minimise any disturbance. The Hillphones service provides daily updates (by recorded message) on stalking activities in the Highlands, and how these might affect walkers. The relevant numbers are: Glen Falloch 01499 600137; Glen Dochart 01567 820886; Grey Corries/Mamores 01855 831511.

The National Park

The Loch Lomond and Trossachs National Park, the first of its kind in Scotland, was officially designated in 2002. It covers a wide area stretching from Loch Earn in the east to Cowal in the west and from Balloch up to Crianlarich. There is a park information centre at Balmaha where further information can be found.

The National Park includes a substantial section of the West Highland Way, and the management of this part of the route has been taken over by the Park authorities, working closely with the local authorities and other interested organisations.

The four aims of the National Park are:

- To conserve and enhance the natural and cultural heritage
- To promote the sustainable use of the natural resources of the area
- To promote understanding and enjoyment (including in the form of recreation) of the special qualities of the area by the public; and
- To promote sustainable social and economic development of the communities of the area.

More information can be found on the Park's website at *www.lochlomond-trossachs.org.*

USEFUL ADDRESSES

GENERAL ENQUIRIES AND ACCOMMODATION

VisitScotland (the Scottish Tourist Board), 23 Ravelston Terrace, Edinburgh EH4 3EE (0845 2255 121, email: *info@visitscotland.com*, website: *www.visitscotland.com*).

Tourist Information Centres

Glasgow—170 Buchanan Street, Glasgow G1 2LW (0141 204 4400, *Glasgow@visitscotland.com*). *Covers Milngavie-Drymen.* Open all year.

National Park Visitor Centre, Balmaha G63 0JQ (01389 722100, *info@west-highland-way.co.uk*). *Covers Drymen-Bridge of Orchy.* Open Easter to October.

Tyndrum—Main Street (01838 400246, *tyndrum@ visitscotland.com*). Open daily March-October.

Fort William—Cameron Square, PH33 6AJ (01397 701801, *fortwilliam@visitscotland.com*). Open all year. *Covers Rannoch Moor-Fort William.*

There is an excellent route website giving a great deal of useful information at *www.west-highland-way.co.uk*.

TRAVEL ENQUIRIES

Traveline 0871 200 22 33 (7am-10pm every day) or *www.travelinescotland.com*.

National rail enquiries line: 08457 48 49 50. ScotRail timetable information can be found on *www. firstgroup.com/scotrail*.

Scottish Citylink Coaches, Buchanan Street Bus Station, Buchanan Street, Glasgow G1 (08705 50 50 50, *www.citylink.co.uk*). For bus services from Glasgow to Fort William.

FERRIES ON LOCH LOMOND

For Rowardennan to Tarbet and Luss, Balmaha to Luss

and Inversnaid to Tarbet, contact Cruise Loch Lomond, 01301 702356, *enquiries@cruiselochlomond.co.uk*. For Inversnaid to Inveruglas, contact the Inversnaid Hotel on 01877 386223 or *www.inversnaid.com*.

WEATHER

There are regular forecasts on BBC Radio Scotland, 92-95khz FM or 810 on medium wave. If you have internet access it is also worth checking the Mountain Weather Information Service (*www.mwis.org.uk*).

COUNTRYSIDE RANGER SERVICES

Countryside Rangers operate along the Way. As well as footpath monitoring and liaising with other land users, they will gladly provide advice and information to walkers and potential walkers. Contact:

East Dunbartonshire and Mugdock Country Park Ranger Service, Craigend Visitor Centre, Mugdock Country Park, Craigallian Road, Milngavie G62 8EL (0141 956 6586, *rangers@mugdock.org*).

Loch Lomond and the Trossachs National Park Rangers, Balmaha G63 0JQ (01389 722100, *info@ west-highland-way.co.uk*).

National Trust for Scotland, Ben Lomond Ranger Service, Ardess Lodge, Rowardennan (0844 493 2217, *benlomond@nts.org.uk*).

Countryside Ranger Service, Highland Council, Ionad Nibheis, Glen Nevis, Fort William PH33 6PF (01397 705922, *westhighlandway@highland.gov.uk*).

ORGANISED HOLIDAYS

A number of companies offer organised and/or guided walks on the West Highland Way. For details please see the *Way Pocket Companion*, available at tourist information centres or from the ranger service addresses above. There are also companies shown in the Pocket Companion offering baggage-carrying and accommodation booking services. This mini-guide also includes full listings for accommodation along the Way and much helpful advice.

WALKERS' COMMENTS

The West Highland Way Management Group welcomes comments from walkers. If you would like to make any comments on the West Highland Way, please write to West Highland Way Management Group, Loch Lomond and The Trossachs National Park, Carrochan, 20 Carrochan Road, Balloch G83 8EG (or email to *whwmailbox@lochlomond-trossachs.org*).

The timeless beauty of Loch Lomond.

INTRODUCTION

The West Highland Way was the first long distance footpath to be established in Scotland under the provisions of the Countryside (Scotland) Act of 1967. The Way runs for 154 km (96 miles) from Milngavie northwards to Fort William – from the outskirts of Scotland's largest city to the foot of its highest mountain, along the shores of its largest loch and across its grandest moor. The West Highland Way is, however, much more than a linking of these topographical superlatives: it is a magnificent walk of very varied character through some of the finest scenery of lowland and highland, mountain and loch, woodland and moorland that Scotland has to show. It provides walking which is in parts pleasant and relaxing, in parts strenuous and rough, in parts remote and exposed to the elements.

The Way mirrors the great evolution of landscape taste in the eighteenth and nineteenth centuries, to which we owe our present enthusiasm for natural scenery. It moves from the urban and domestic in lowland Central Scotland, through the romantic and picturesque in Loch Lomond and Glen Falloch, to the savage and sublime in Rannoch and Lochaber. In this passage from Lowlands to Highlands, the walker on the Way experiences sharp contrasts in geology and landforms, in flora and fauna, and in the human patterns of land use and settlement. Everywhere in the country around the route there are the traces of human history; a history dominated by tensions and conflicts between two cultures, but also coloured by trade and traffic between them.

In fact much of the West Highland Way follows ancient and historic routes. It makes use of the old footpaths of the Highlanders, and the drove roads by which they herded their cattle southwards to Lowland markets in a trade which was still active a century ago. It makes extensive use of the eighteenth-century military roads, built largely by troops to help control the Jacobite clansmen. It uses old coaching roads and farm roads in the Lowlands; and it follows the course of railway lines where trains ran not so very long ago.

Substantial stretches of the Way have always been open to the walker as public rights of way, and have been enjoyed by generations of outdoor enthusiasts; but the virtue of the route's official designation and creation has been to link these together into a coherent entity of great character: the total is considerably more than the sum of its parts. Thus, while many fine short sections are readily accessible by car or by public transport, for maximum enjoyment the West Highland Way should be walked as a whole, or at least in substantial sections. Only by this approach can the walker fully appreciate the wealth of landscape contrast and achieve the genuine sense of travel that the Way offers.

The idea of a long-distance footpath from Glasgow northwards had its origins far back in the Glasgow tramping and climbing tradition; elements of the West Highland Way can be identified in outdoor magazines of the 1930s and 40s. However, the concept of the route began to crystallise in the late 1960s, with Tom Stephenson's Pennine Way in England as a precedent, and the Countryside (Scotland) Act of 1967 as the means of realisation. There was a happy co-ordination of activity between the outdoor interests and government agencies. During 1969 the Glasgow Group of the Holiday Fellowship, and other clubs, under the enthusiastic direction of Tom Hunter, undertook much survey work on a potential footpath northwards from Glasgow, while at the end of that year the Scottish Development Department commissioned F.J. Evans to make an examination and report on 'A Footpath System North of Glasgow'. The results of the Glasgow Group's survey were generously made available to Mr Evans, whose report endorsed their proposal for a long-distance route from Glasgow as far as Glen Falloch, the northern half being outwith his immediate remit. He called it 'Highland Footway'.

After considering this report, the Countryside Commission for Scotland decided to investigate the potential route in detail. In 1972, after much fieldwork, the Commission submitted its study report for the route, now called 'The West Highland Way', to the local authorities who would be concerned with its implementation. In the light of its consultations with these authorities, the Commission at the end of 1973 submitted a revised report to the Secretary of State for Scotland for his approval, which was given in September 1974. It is a tribute to the work of the outdoor clubs' working party that the Way was approved very much along the line their survey had suggested.

The implementation of the Way – the negotiation with proprietors over access agreements and the details of the route, the

provision of bridges, gates and stiles, waymarking and information boards – was a longer, slower process than anyone would
have wished. Soon after the Secretary of State had given his
approval, the reorganisation of local government in Scotland
transformed the implementing authorities from five old counties
into three new Regions – Strathclyde, Central and Highland.
Inevitably, considerable changes in organisational structures,
areas of responsibility and staff, led to a loss of continuity and
momentum in implementation. Shortly thereafter, economic
cuts reduced the manpower and finance available to carry the
work forward.

From 1978 to 1980, however, the Countryside Commission
for Scotland and the local authorities took determined steps to
bring the route to reality. With help from units of the Regular
and Territorial Army, from work parties of the British Trust for
Conservation Volunteers, and from Forestry Commission staff,
work on bridges, drainage, path-cutting and waymarking made
steady progress. The West Highland Way was officially opened at

June foxgloves along the Way.

Balmaha on 6 October 1980 by Lord Mansfield, then Minister of State at the Scottish Office.

The Silver Jubilee of the route was celebrated in 2005 with a relay involving 1,000 children and young people. This and other events were supported by local and national politicians and celebrities, culminating in a presence of representatives before the Queen. The popularity of the West Highland Way continues to grow and there are now around 15,000 people completing the route each year and an additional 80,000 doing parts of it.

The income generated from walkers, cyclists, horse-riders and holidaymakers helps to support over 200 businesses and contributes in the region of £3.5 million per annum to the Scottish economy. As tourism takes over from agriculture as the main employer in areas on and adjacent to the Way, the social and economic impacts of the route should not be underestimated. The Way has significantly contributed to the regeneration of some of the small communities in the Scottish Highlands through employment opportunities, business development and commercial enterprise.

The West Highland Way has become an internationally significant icon of some of the best Scotland has to offer – magnificent scenery, rich culture, amazing wildlife, unrivalled hospitality, challenge and adventure. The walking surface, infrastructure, interpretation and supporting literature have all been greatly improved, but the experience of walking the Way remains as it always has been, a classic backpacking excursion through some of the finest scenery in Scotland.

Try it for yourself: you will not be disappointed.

The Clyde, Kelvin and Allander
Walkways

These three linked paths provide a pleasant walking route from the centre of Glasgow to the official start of the West Highland Way at Milngavie, and an alternative to taking the train. The route is about 19km in length and is waymarked throughout. There are numerous points of access along the way.

From the city centre, make your way down to the river and turn west. The Clyde Walkway passes the Finnieston Crane and the Scottish Exhibition and Conference Centre before meeting the Kelvin, where the route turns north. Little remains of the once-great shipbuilding industry on the Clyde, where so many superb ships were launched. The Finnieston Crane, affectionately known as Big Finn, still stands by the river to remind us of the tremendous achievements of the past.

The walkway passes close to the Kelvin Hall, where Glasgow's Transport Museum is housed; the Kelvingrove Art Galleries and Museum, home to many important collections; Kelvingrove Park; Glasgow University; and the Botanic Gardens, with the fairytale Kibble Palace. Further north the walkway passes through Maryhill and crosses the line of the Antonine Wall, built by the Romans in AD 142, at about the site of the Brasher Bridge, constructed with funding from the Chris Brasher Trust. Shortly after this, as the Kelvin turns east, the route swings west along the Allander Water, which rises in the Kilpatrick Hills and runs for about 9 km to its confluence with the Kelvin. The walkway continues to Milngavie Station, where the West Highland Way can be picked up.

The walkways were developed by Strathclyde Regional Council, Bearsden & Milngavie District Council and the City of Glasgow District Council, with assistance from the European Regional Development Fund. They have been replaced by East Dunbartonshire Council, Stirling Council and City of Glasgow Council, who are now taking forward the work and improvements on this section. A leaflet giving fuller details is available at tourist information centres and other local outlets.

1
Milngavie – Drymen

SUMMARY

Distance: 19.5 km (12 miles).

Height range: 80-140 m. **Total ascent**: 245 m.

Accommodation: Hotels and B&Bs in Milngavie and Drymen. Wigwam shelters at Drumquhassle Farm.

Supplies: Reasonable range of shops in Milngavie and Drymen.

Public transport: Regular train and bus services from Glasgow to Milngavie. Reasonable bus service from Drymen, and also from Strathblane.

Terrain summary: This section provides a relatively simple start to the Way on footpaths, tracks, lanes and an old railway with no major climbs. The route is accessible by car at numerous points. An easy day's walk.

The obelisk marking the start of the Way.

1

Lennox

From its beginning in Milngavie, north-west of Glasgow, to Inverarnan at the head of Loch Lomond, the West Highland Way runs through the ancient province and earldom of Lennox. At one time, Lennox included all the country between the Campsie Fells in the east and Loch Long in the west, and between the River Clyde and the foot of Glen Falloch. For the purposes of the Guide, the long stretch of the Way along the shore of Loch Lomond, which is such a major element of the route, has a chapter to itself. This Lennox chapter therefore takes the Way over the ridge north of Milngavie, through Strathblane and Strathendrick, and by the forest of Garadhban and the hills of the Highland edge to Loch Lomond. This is the main Lowland part of the West Highland Way, a gentle country of farmland and woodland. The name Lennox is generally taken to be a Latinised corruption of 'Levenachen', meaning a place of elm trees. It comes from the same root as Leven, which was the old name for Loch Lomond and is still the name of the river by which the loch drains to the Clyde.

The name of Lennox is a thread that runs throughout the fabric of Scottish history. The Earldom of Lennox was conferred upon Alwyn Marcarkyl by King Malcolm IV of Scotland in 1153. The Lennox family soon became a force to be reckoned with in feudal Scotland; the fifth Earl, Malcolm, was a staunch supporter of Robert the Bruce during the Wars of Independence, and a signatory to the Declaration of Arbroath in 1320. By the end of the 14th century, the Earls had achieved the fullest extent of their landholding and influence, in a country torn by strife between rival nobles. They then brought about their own downfall by a marriage link with the powerful Dukes of Albany, the nominal Governors of Scotland during the long captivity in England of James I; for on James' return, he made a strong show of his royal authority by summarily executing Albany and the aged Earl Duncan of Lennox at Stirling in 1425. These events provided John Galt with the framework for his historical novel *The Spaewife*.

Earl Duncan left no male heirs. After half a century of internal wrangling over the succession, the earldom of Lennox was arrogated by the Darnley Stewarts in 1488. This family, as close relatives of the Stuart kings, played an important role in every tempestuous reign until the Union of the Crowns in 1603, achieving a short-lived zenith of power in the marriage of Henry, Lord Darnley, to Mary Queen of Scots, before he was murdered.

The direct line of descent died out in 1672 when the title and lands of Lennox fell to Charles II, who promptly conferred them, with the Dukedom of Richmond, upon an illegitimate son. In 1702 he in turn sold the estates to the Marquis of Montrose, whose family, the Grahams, had held lands in Lennox – mainly at Mugdock and Carbeth – since the thirteenth century. The Dukes of Montrose thus became the most substantial landowners in Lennox, and retained that distinction until after the First World War.

Milngavie – Carbeth
(7 km: 4.25 miles)

THE West Highland Way begins with an appealing directness. Its start lies less than 10 km from the heart of Scotland's largest city, at a commuter railway station close by a bustling shopping centre; but after a few hundred metres the Way passes out of the urban environment into countryside which rapidly opens out as you head north. As the sardonic old saying puts it, 'Glasgow is a good place to get out of' – the city is close-ringed by fine hill and moorland country. With this rural hinterland, Glasgow has always had a strong outdoor tradition, and Milngavie has long been one of the most popular starting points for outings to the countryside. It is very appropriate that the West Highland Way, which in its early evolution was fostered by the Glasgow outdoor fraternity, should begin its northward course at Milngavie.

Assuming that you are starting from Glasgow city centre, it is easy to reach the start of the Way. A frequent train service operates from Queen Street or Central Stations, though it may be necessary to change at Partick. There is a regular bus service to Milngavie from Buchanan Street bus station. You can also walk out to Milngavie, using the Clyde, Kelvin and Allander Walkways – see page xxxv for details.

When asking directions or buying tickets, visitors can avoid confusion and perhaps some amusement at their expense by remembering that Milngavie is pronounced approximately

'Mull-guy'. It has been suggested that the name derives from the Gaelic *Muileann-gaoithe*, meaning a windmill. The name appears on seventeenth century maps as Milguy, and its anglicisation appears to be relatively recent. The down-to-earth Glaswegian humour ascribes it to Milngavie's rather 'upper-class' image and a wit of the 1920s declared:

> 'Yet I have heard that in Milngavie,
> The folk are quite reserved and shy,
> And every house has got a slavey,
> Who's taught to call the place Milngavie.'

As late as the 1790s, however, Milngavie was a tiny village of about 200 people, owing its livelihood to the Allander Water which supplied the power for several mills, including a snuffmill and a paper mill, as well as water for the bleaching of textiles. In common with many other towns in the West of Scotland, Milngavie grew with the cotton industry, and by 1835 its population had increased six-fold.

As well as the railway station, there are bus stops and ample car-parking facilities nearby. From the station a pedestrian underpass leads up a flight of steps into Station Road, which after about 150 metres continues into Douglas Street. This pedestrian precinct offers a range of shops, banks, cafes and restaurants. Since there is no comparable shopping centre on the Way before Fort William, you might like to take the opportunity to top up any supplies you need here.

The Way leaves Douglas Street at the bridge over the Allander Water. At a granite obelisk unveiled in 1992, marking the official start point, it runs down a walkway ramp over the stream, northwards around a small car-park at the rear of the shops. Here you will find a landscaped area with seating, a plaque commemorating the 25th anniversary of the Way in 2005, and the first of a number of interpretation panels that reveal some of the historical journeys that took place along what is now the route of the West Highland Way. From here the route crosses a road and continues along a tarmac path for 100 metres or so. It then passes under another road to enter a sunken, tree-lined lane on the line of an old railway that served a former paper mill on the Allander Water. As this lane heads north, the noise and bustle of the town rapidly recede.

In Mugdock Park.

Shortly after it passes the Milngavie Community Education Centre and Library on the left, the Way leaves the former railway, turning left and right to the Allander Water. It follows the east bank of the stream through wooded parkland for 400 metres or so before striking rightwards and uphill away from the riverbank, climbing gradually to the upper part of Allander Park, a rough moorland of birch, heather and gorse above the town.

From near the crest of this rise there is a good view southwards over the suburban fringes of Glasgow, and westwards along the front of the Kilpatrick hills. The ridge on which you now stand, and which the Way crosses as it heads north, is part of the same geological formation as the Kilpatricks and the Campsie Fells, although they are a good deal higher. All were formed by great lava flows in the Lower Carboniferous period, some 350 million years ago, which may originally have covered as much as 1,500 square km (600 sq. miles) and have been well over 600 metres (2,000 feet) thick. Despite having been much eroded and faulted over time, these Clyde Plateau Lavas still appear as upstanding hill masses in the Central 'Lowlands' of Scotland. A conspicuous feature of the formation is the 'tiered' effect created by successive lava flows, which is well seen in the face of the Campsies above Strathblane, and in looking back to the Kilpatricks from the Drymen area.

5

THE WEST HIGHLAND WAY

The Way now turns left (north-eastwards) over an open moor of bracken and birch to follow a long ride, the former drive to Craigallian House, through Mugdock Wood. Mugdock is a long-established oak wood, notable for its bluebells. Here in spring and summer you will find many of the small grassland flowers that grow along much of the length of the West Highland Way. One of the brightest and most prolific is the little yellow tormentil, but others, so common that even non-botanists will quickly come to recognise them, include the heath bedstraw, with clusters of tiny white flowers, and the delicate blue milkwort. In ditches and damper places the pink lousewort and the purplish pom-pom of the scabious are common. There, too, you will find the butterwort, a violet flower hanging gracefully on a tall stem that rises from a flat rosette of yellow-green leaves. The leaves curl up to catch and digest small insects. Where the ground is very wet the sundew takes over the insectivorous role, with round red leaf-pads covered in sticky hairs to entrap flies.

In 1980 Mugdock Wood, together with land to the north-east, around the ancient ruin of Mugdock Castle, was gifted by Sir Hugh Fraser to provide a Country Park for the people of Glasgow. The park is run by the Mugdock Management Committee on behalf of East Dumbartonshire and Stirling Councils – the boundary between council areas follows the southern edge of Mugdock Wood and the Allander Water. It includes an area of oak woodland (a Site of Special Scientific Interest), the ruins of two castles and an

Craigallian Loch.

attractive loch. The Visitor Centre is signposted from the Way, and includes a café, restaurant and toilets. There are several car parks, picnic sites and a network of footpaths and bridleways. The park has its own website at *www.mugdock-country-park.org.uk*.

At the end of the old drive through the wood, the Way turns leftwards down a minor road (known locally as the Khyber Pass) for a few metres, then resumes its course, turning right through a gate onto a track winding along the rushy flats by the Allander Burn and up the west shore of Craigallian Loch. On this stretch you will have your first view of Dumgoyne, the hunchback, knobbly hill at the western end of the Campsies, which dominates the Way through Strathblane and remains visible far to the north. The West Highland Way is favoured with a succession of these 'mountain mileposts', hills of distinctive character by which you can measure progress, and which change their aspect as you pass. Dumgoyne is the first of them, and one of the finest despite its modest height of 427 metres (1,402 feet).

Craigallian Loch lies in a shallow scoop through the ridge between Milngavie and Strathblane, probably cut by an arm of the great glacier that flowed southwards through Strathblane from the Highland icefields during the last glaciation. The rough, wooded hill-slopes around the loch have been well-known as a weekend escape for generations of Glaswegians, from Victorian and Edwardian naturalists to the thousands of Boy Scouts who have over the years used the nearby camp at Auchengillan.

It was, however, during the Depression years of the 1930s that Craigallian achieved its apotheosis, in 'The Fire' – a bonfire on the slopes above the loch where weekenders and unemployed men met, ate, gossiped and sang. There are many stirring tales of the tough characters and rough living of those days; of men who, unable to afford sleeping-bags, slept in brown paper or under the *Glasgow Herald* – which they preferred to other newspapers not for the quality of its journalism but for the size of its pages; of fights on wet dark nights for the restricted comforts of a telephone kiosk; of epic journeys by lorry or motor-bike to tackle desperate climbs with primitive equipment. For these folk there will always be a certain magic in the Craigallian area, where later comers see only the spruce plantation above the loch.

There is further evidence of the escape to the country in the

The approach to Dumgoyne.

little holiday huts around the Way where it goes down to the right beyond the gate at the plantation's edge. These are only a fraction of the 140 or so huts scattered around the hill to the west, on the Carbeth estate; all were built before or shortly after the Second World War, when planning regulations were less stringent than they are now, and it is a tribute to the loving care and effort devoted to their maintenance that so many remain. At the time of writing (early 2013) the Carbeth community of 'hutters' were trying to raise £1.75 million to buy the land and manage it themselves.

The Way crosses the outflow from Carbeth Loch, then goes up to join an estate driveway a short distance before it meets the B821 road at a gateway which rejoices in the name of Ballachalairy Yett – 'yett' being an old Scots word for 'gate'. The Way goes west for about 300 metres to where a gate on the right leads into the 'Tinker's Loan', a broad ride between parallel stone dykes, rising with an attractive air of expectancy to a gate on the skyline, with the Campsie Fells beyond it. The name and appearance of this ride indicate that it is an old roadway, probably dating back to the days before enclosure of the fields.

The crest at the head of the Loan, though unspectacular in itself, marks an important early stage in the Way. It is the edge of the Glasgow basin or 'howe', the watershed from which the streams drain northwards and westwards into Loch Lomond, and from which the Way descends again to only a few metres above sea-level. In clear weather this – or perhaps a point a little further down to the north – is one of the Way's finer viewpoints, the wide vista to the north being enclosed by the Kilpatricks on the one hand and the rugged scarp of the Campsies on the other. The immediate foreground is rather rough, but is offset by the steep wooded knoll of Dumgoyach and the fertile chequerboard of the Lennox plains, with the Highland edge beyond. In good visibility the horizon shows a long frieze of mountains, from Ben Ledi on the right, round to the far Crianlarich hills, but your eye will probably settle on the broad-shouldered bulk of Ben Lomond, towards the left, another mountain milepost marking the first quarter of the distance to Fort William. You are now well started on the Way.

Carbeth – Drymen
(12.5 km; 7.75 miles)

Please note that dogs must be kept on leads on this section.

THE stretch of the Way from the ridgecrest at Carbeth to the A811 road near Drymen is the most pleasantly domestic part of the whole route, and passes through its richest farmland. As you descend into Strathblane, you may well feel inclined to agree with the author of the *Old Statistical Account* at the end of the eighteenth century, who suggested that the visitor would here be charmed with 'the verdure of the country, the mildness of the air, and the appearance of cheerfulness and plenty, which is displayed around... In summer, the landscape is enriched and adorned by the luxuriant foliage of the woods with which the hills are skirted...'

There are also signs of a long human occupation. The cottages of Arlehaven, which the Way skirts before it turns left towards Dumgoyach, are relatively modern; but the lands of 'Erleleven', as part of the estates of Duntreath, were granted by King James I to his brother-in-law William Edmonstone around 1434, after the King had broken the power of the Earls of Lennox. The grant was

9

confirmed in 1452 by James II, who further elevated the estate into the Barony of Duntreath. The 'reddendo' or token rental for these lands, to be produced on demand at Duntreath 'at the feast of the nativity of John the Baptist', was one pound of pepper; the lands are still held by the Edmonstone family today.

Again, as the Way descends over what used to be rather boggy ground on the slopes below Arlehaven – where you may find among the rushes such fine marsh flowers as the austere white grass of Parnassus – it passes, on the ridge to your right, the Dumgoyach Standing Stones. These five large boulders, aligned roughly north-west to south-east, are thought to date back to Neolithic times, when the open ground above Strathblane may have offered easier cultivation than the valley floor, which would probably have been ill-drained and densely wooded. Radio-carbon dating

Dumgoyach.

of charcoal found there during an excavation in 1972 suggested a date around 3,500BC. The Stones have limited interest for close examination, and you can best contribute to their conservation by viewing them from a distance.

The remarkably steep, wooded cone of Dumgoyach, which the Way turns on its west flank, is one of the remnant volcanoes from which the Clyde Plateau lavas emerged – that is, the resistant neck through which the lavas flowed upwards and outwards in successive layers. Dumgoyach is almost pure basalt, while other similar necks like Dumgoyne and Dumfoyne, the less distinctive bump to the south-east of Dumgoyne, contain basalt agglomerates: they show remaining fragments of the rock through which the volcanic vent pushed its way. The Campsies present a fine steep rampart above Strathblane, and can be approached by several routes from the valley. The basalt crags on the hill fronts should be avoided, for the rock is as a rule extremely friable and loose.

The Way goes round the west side of Dumgoyach Farm, down a lane and along the farm road to cross the Blane Water by a plank bridge. Just beyond the bridge, it turns left on to the old track of the Blane Valley railway line, which it follows for the next 6.5 km (4 miles) to near Gartness. As might be expected, the former railway line gives pleasant and easy walking, especially in dry conditions: after rain it can be rather muddy. It is crossed by a substantial number of farm access lanes, and a succession of gates or metal V-stiles at each will slow you somewhat.

The Blane Valley Railway was opened to passengers in 1867, as far as Killearn Station – later Dumgoyne Station – where the Way now crosses the A81 road for the first time; in 1882 it was extended northwards to Aberfoyle. The promoters had hoped that Glasgow's wealthier businessmen would build their houses in Strathblane and commute to the city by railway, but the line was a circuitous one and traffic was always light. Not surprisingly it was one of the early casualties of post-war rationalisation of the railways. Passenger services were withdrawn in 1951, and the line closed completely in 1959.

However, even before its adoption for the West Highland Way, the old Blane Valley line had taken on a new lease of life as a routeway for the 1,520 mm (60-inch) water pipeline which is used by Scottish Water to transport water from Loch Lomond

11

Blane Water.

to consumers throughout Central Scotland, including some as far away as Livingston in West Lothian. It is this buried pipeline that forms the raised embankment along the old railway track. This convenient route in the valley bottom contrasts with the line taken by the much older pipeline that carries Glasgow's water supply from its main source at Loch Katrine in the Trossachs: it runs along the hillside some way above the A81.

In fact the great flat-bottomed trench of Strathblane provides an excellent natural route through the hill ranges on either side. The valley is the product of a variety of geological factors and is clearly not the result of erosion by the relatively small Blane Water. It is partly a fault-controlled valley, the southern fault being represented in the steep brae below Arlehaven; geologists argue that it may be a remnant of an ancient river system that once drained south-eastwards towards the Forth estuary.

Certainly the strath was further eroded by ice during the Pleistocene glaciation, and it has been suggested that the valley's flat floor represents the sandy bed of a lake trapped by an ice-sheet that blocked the northwards drainage as the Highland ice retreated. As evidence of the character of the valley floor, you will notice not only the fertility of its soil, but also the absence of dykes as field boundaries, due to the lack of boulders or rock outcrops.

As the Way continues under the craggy shoulders of Dumgoyne, it passes on the right the distillery and bond warehouses of Glengoyne, which has been producing malt whisky for nearly a century and a half. It was formerly known as Glenguin, a name which has passed into the peerage, for that was the title taken by Lord Tedder, Marshal of the Royal Air Force, who was born in one of the houses uphill from the distillery in 1890. Tedder achieved great success in partnerships with Generals Auchinleck and Alexander in the Western Desert campaigns of World War Two, before going on to act as Deputy Supreme Commander in Europe to General Eisenhower from 1943 to 1945; he died in 1967.

The distillery is open to visitors, and a signpost on the Way indicates a path across to it. It is open all year, with regular conducted tours (Mar-Nov 10.00-16.00, Dec-Feb 10.00-15.00. Tours last 45 minutes and include a tasting). The diversion to see how whisky is produced is well worth while if you have the time. Further details from www.glengoyne.com. You can also get a bus back to Milngavie or Glasgow from outside the distillery.

Two other famous men are associated with the Strathblane area, or more precisely with the parish of Killearn, which lies between this point and the River Endrick. George Buchanan and John Napier both made major contributions to the European Renaissance, though in very different fields. Napier is now the better

Glengoyne Distillery.

known of the two, for his work was largely in mathematics, and he is credited with the invention of logarithms. He lived at various times at Gartness Castle, which stood by the Endrick some way further north. Buchanan – scholar, philosopher and poet, tutor to James VI of Scotland and I of England – was born at the humble farmstead of Moss, which may be seen half-hidden in trees south-west of the Way a few hundred metres after it crosses the busy A81 at the former Dumgoyne station. The original house is long gone, but at the road crossing is the Beech Tree Inn, which offers food and drink all day and has a 'walkers' garden' outside where you are welcome to eat your own food provided you buy a drink (*www.thebeechtreeinn.co.uk*).

George Buchanan (1506–82) lived in troubled times, both in Scotland during the hectic reign of Mary Queen of Scots, and in Europe, where he travelled widely, as the Reformation ran its course. However, Buchanan's huge contemporary reputation, based on his mastery of Latin, the lingua franca of the Renaissance, has dwindled away almost to vanishing point as the study of Latin has declined, while the name of Napier (1550–1617), his near contemporary, has grown with the growth of mathematics as a discipline. However, George Buchanan was not forgotten by his countrymen, who erected a large obelisk to his memory in Killearn village in 1788. You can catch a glimpse of this monument from higher points a little further north along the Way.

In this vicinity the Way goes through a rather semi-urban phase, as it passes successively a small factory, the Killearn sewage plant, and a garage, while it parallels the main road. A little further on, across the road, is the site of Killearn Hospital, covering around 20 hectares. The hospital was built prior to the Second World War as an emergency unit to treat the expected casualties of bombing raids on the Glasgow conurbation, and for nearly 30 years after the war it served as a specialist neuro-surgical unit before closing in 1972. Most of the site has now been cleared.

Just beyond the hospital site the Way passes under the B834, which incidentally leads eastwards within 1.5 km to Killearn, a quiet village given a new lease of life in recent years by an influx of Glasgow commuters, and offering a range of shops and some accommodation. There is now a clear sense of having moved into a new province, out of the narrower views of Strathblane, a sense

Views of the Strathblane hills from the Way.

confirmed as the old railway rises gradually to cross the A81 road for the second time. This higher ground offers wide prospects east along the northern front of the Campsies, west across the open farmland of Strathendrick, and north to the Highland edge. As if in confirmation of the change of scene, the topography also changes, swelling in soft rolling ridges that stretch from here on to Drymen. These are the remains of a great sheet of sand and gravel laid down at the front of an ice-lobe which flowed down the valley of Loch Lomond to sprawl outwards across the piedmont plain of Lennox in the final readvance of the last glaciation, only some 12,000 years ago. Conic Hill is visible, and in clear conditions the summit of Ben Lomond can be seen.

About 750 metres after crossing the A81, the Way finally leaves the old Blane Valley railway. It turns left by a bridge and continues on the minor road from Killearn to Drymen, a short distance from Gartness. This is a pleasant, rambling country lane, but you should be wary of traffic, particularly at bends and on narrower sections.

From the railway the road dips gently down to cross the River Endrick by the douce hamlet of Gartness, a little terrace of cot-

15

tages facing the river with no two houses quite alike. The starkly functional modern bridge of 1971 replaced an old one dating from 1715; in the autumn it provides an excellent platform from which to view salmon leaping up the rapids on their way to spawning grounds in the headwaters of the Endrick. Beneath the bridge the river courses over great slabby ledges, the beds of the Old Red Sandstone. These rocks of Devonian age floor the wide valley between the Highland edge and the volcanic plateaux of the Campsies and the Kilpatricks. As the Gartness cottages show, the sandstone makes a pleasant, warm building stone.

The old mill lade under the bridge hints at past activity. A few hundred metres down-river there are ruins of other mills; one of them incorporates stones from the medieval Gartness Castle, which once stood nearby, though nothing of it now remains. The lands of Gartness passed into the hands of the Napier family, who also held the estate of Merchiston, near Edinburgh, during the fifteenth-century squabbles over the Earldom of Lennox, to which the Napiers, like the Darnley Stewarts, had a claim by marriage.

It was at Gartness Castle that John Napier, the philosopher and mathematician, is said to have stayed on occasion. According to tradition he had many of the attributes of an absentminded professor; he would order the watermill to be shut off when its creaking machinery disturbed his studies, and he was inclined to wander about the Endrick banks at night in his nightgown and cap, lost in thought. Not surprisingly, local folk were firmly of the opinion that he was a warlock in league with the Devil.

Following the road (which also becomes part of Sustrans Cycle Route 7), the Way climbs west to the top of the ridge by Upper Gartness Farm, crossing the route of the Forth and Clyde Junction Railway. Opened in 1856 to link Stirling and the Vale of Leven, it was never much more than a useful farmers' line with some seasonal tourist traffic. This section was closed to passengers as long ago as 1934 and is now a rich, tangled corridor of birchwood, gorse and bramble.

The top of the hill by Upper Gartness gives an excellent panorama over the fertile farmland of Strathendrick, with the river winding against high banks cut into the fluvio-glacial deposits. The north face of the Campsie Fells shows a rugged front in which volcanic necks stand out as resistant craggy buttresses separating

Mature natural woodland along the Way.

deep-sculpted corries. Dumgoyach stands sentinel at the head of Strathblane, and to the west and north the hills around Loch Lomond begin to assert their individuality: the little crag-and-tail of Duncryne above Gartocharn, well-known as the personal viewpoint of the late Tom Weir, climber, author and naturalist; the shapely Luss Hills above the Loch's west shore; and the knobbly ridge of Conic Hill above Balmaha, your next milestone. Conic Hill marks the line of the great Highland Boundary Fault that runs from near Helensburgh on the Clyde, to Stonehaven on the east coast, and so divides Highlands from Lowlands, at least in geological terms.

As the Way follows the minor road along the Drumquhassle ridge towards Drymen, the contrast between the rolling patchwork of farmland and hedgerow on either hand, and the moorland and forest to the north becomes more evident. The Romans built a small fort here as part of a chain of frontier posts along the Highland edge. No trace remains above ground level, and though the existence of a fort hereabouts was long suspected – even the corrupt placename Drumquhassle, 'castle ridge', may refer to it – only aerial photography revealed the site. But the proximity of the Highlands to the rich lands of Lennox and Menteith kept the area in a state of constant anxiety well into the eighteenth century.

17

Its herds of fat cattle and flocks of sheep lay at the mercy of raids and incursions from the more lawless Highland clans, of whom the most notorious were the MacGregors living around the heads of Loch Lomond and Loch Katrine.

The depredations inflicted on the hapless Lowland farmers were so regular, and the forces of law and order so impotent against the reivers, that the MacGregors and others were able to turn their activities from a high-risk enterprise with irregular and unpredictable returns into a rather more secure trading arrangement with guaranteed income. In modern terms, they went into a protection racket. In return for payment of blackmail by the landholders most at risk, they guaranteed to prevent the theft of cattle and damage to property by Highland caterans, and to recover or make restitution for losses suffered. Since most of the raids had been conducted by themselves, it was not difficult to stop them: but it does seem that the blackmail contracts were honoured on most occasions, when other malefactors were pursued – sometimes far into the Highlands – and made to give up their spoils.

To modern eyes the legal formality of the surviving contracts, with their attested signatures, penalty clauses, and carefully fixed rates of payment – in one example £4 per year per £100 valuation of a farmer's landholding – has a slightly absurd quality. For the suffering Lowland farmers, however, there was no humour in the situation. They were caught between the Devil and the deep blue sea, for the civil authorities, while almost powerless to control the MacGregors, prohibited any sort of treatying with them and threatened to take stern measures against the signatories of blackmail contracts. For all that, the authorities themselves would on occasion contract with the MacGregors to provide a force, dignified by the title of 'The Watch', to prevent raids and incursions. The famous Rob Roy served in such a 'legal' Watch as a young man.

At Easter Drumquhassle – which also provides B&B – you will find the first of the chain of wooden 'wigwams' provided along the West Highland Way in 1995. These simple shelters were designed by Charles Gulland to use available local timber, making them easy and inexpensive to erect. They offer low-cost accommodation on a sleeping platform; a form of indoor camping, if you like.

From the road on the crest of the ridge there is a glimpse of the lower part of Loch Lomond and some of its wooded islands over the policies of Buchanan Castle, the former residence of the Dukes of Montrose ('policies' is a Scottish term for the grounds or parkland of a large house). The road gradually descends past the plantation of Gateside on the right; just after it turns west towards Drymen by the entrance to Gateside, an old right-of-way path used by generations of schoolchildren takes the Way north across an open field by a burn and up to the A811 road immediately east of its junction with the B858 to Drymen, and opposite the Drymen Primary School and schoolhouse. These buildings, like those at Gartness, use the warm red local sandstone. You have now entered the Loch Lomond and The Trossachs National Park.

NB: at the time of writing (early 2013) the first part of the route through the Garadhban Forest was closed due to timber operations and storm damage and a signposted diversion was in place taking walkers into Drymen and then out along the minor road to Gartmore. Please follow the diversion signs if they still apply.

The Way here turns east for a short distance along the main road. However, on either the B858 or the minor road at Gateside it is less than a kilometre west to Drymen. This pleasant village centres round a small green, an unusual feature in Scottish rural settlements. As 'Drumyn', from the Gaelic, 'a little ridge', it is first mentioned in a charter of 1238 in which Alwyn, Earl of Lennox, granted lands to Paisley Abbey. It is now a centre from which bus services run to Glasgow, Stirling, Aberfoyle, Balloch at the foot of Loch Lomond, and to Balmaha, where the Way reaches the loch. Walkers wishing to take an easier route can rejoin the West Highland Way in the Garadhban woods north of Drymen by taking the minor road to Gartmore which runs up from the head of the green. This road is also the start of the Rob Roy Way, a trail which runs from Drymen to Pitlochry (see above re diversion).

Drymen offers not only hotel and B&B accommodation, but also a range of shops and services not matched along the Way till Kinlochleven, nearly 100km further north. In particular, the village boasts the last bank to be found in all that distance. Like the travellers of old, Waywalkers will do well to look to their purses before crossing the Highland Line.

2
Drymen – Rowardennan

SUMMARY

Distance: 22.5 km (14 miles).

Height range: 20-358 m. **Total ascent:** 540 m.

Accommodation: Hotels and B&Bs in Drymen. B&Bs in Balmaha. Hotel and youth hostel at Rowardennan.

Services: Reasonable range of shops in Drymen. Small shop in Balmaha. Nothing further north until Inverarnan.

Public transport: Good bus services to Glasgow and Stirling from Drymen. Reasonable service between Drymen and Balmaha. No public transport to Rowardennan apart from the Loch Lomond water bus.

Terrain summary: This section follows good paths or tracks most of the way. The first major climb is over Conic Hill (358 m) near Balmaha. The lochside route to Rowardennan is twisty and surprisingly undulating, with intermittent good views as you wind through the woods. A harder day than it might appear from the map.

Drymen – Balmaha
(10.5 km; 6.5 miles)

Note: as this edition was prepared, there was a substantial diversion in place around the Garadhban Forest due to extensive timber operations and also clearance of windblown trees resulting from storm damage. It is hoped that the diversion will be removed before this edition of the guide is published, but if it is still in place please follow the diversion signs, which are clearly marked on the ground.

From Drymen school the A811 runs eastwards in a purposeful line that contrasts with the ambling farm roads the Way has followed from Gartness. Even if the map did not make it explicit, the straightness of the road over hill and dip would

View of Loch Lomond from Conic Hill.

suggest its origins as an old military road, built soon after the Jacobite Rising of 1745 to link the castles at Stirling and Dumbarton.

As you begin the 10 km (6 mile) stretch to Balmaha, you can be excused for feeling that you are making it hard for yourself, as the next milepost, Conic Hill, recedes behind your left shoulder. However, after about 400 metres along the main road, the Way strikes north opposite the steading of Blarnavaid Farm and climbs steadily by farm and forest track before beginning a long westwards traverse through the Garadhban Forest at around 150 metres (500 feet).

The Forestry Commission's holdings of over 500 hectares (1,300 acres) at Garadhban date back to 1931, so there is some well-established old timber in the plantations. Recent replanting has increased the ecological variety of the forest and created a variety of age-classes in the plantations. As a result these woods are particularly interesting for ornithologists, who may have the luck to see less common bird species such as crossbill or siskin.

THE WEST HIGHLAND WAY

The high quality rural landscape of these lowlands, in which farmland and woodland intermingle to fine effect, owes much to the activity of successive Dukes of Montrose. At the end of the 17th century, the third Marquis of Montrose purchased the estates of Buchanan, and a little later his son, the first Duke, added the substantial remaining estates of Lennox. The family thus came to control the whole east shore of Loch Lomond.

The superbly wooded parklands to the west of Drymen were planted to complement the vast baronial mansion of Buchanan Castle, built between 1854 and 1857 to replace an earlier house destroyed by fire. During the Second World War it served as a military hospital, but thereafter it lay empty and was partly demolished. A large part of the Montrose estates was sold after the death of the fifth Duke in 1925, but much of the finest woodland was preserved, particularly within the Queen Elizabeth Forest Park on Loch Lomondside.

The route through the forest.

At the end of the long traverse the excellent forest roads run out first into a grassy track through young Norway spruce, and then into a well-surfaced path through an old plantation. You cross the track leading up to Moorpark, which provides an opportunity to turn left out to the B837 road if you do not wish to tackle Conic Hill. At the woodland edge the Way passes into rough, bracken-clad moorland pasture, stretching over to the barrier hills of the Highland edge, which seem suddenly close at hand. Leftwards the moor slopes down into farmland and woodland above the levels of Loch Lomond. The contrast with the sheltered enclosure of the Garadhban is sharply invigorating.

The next stretch, at one time difficult to follow in midsummer, when the bracken can reach over head-height in places, is now a fine machine path. Over the moor to the northwest, you keep the dyke on your right as far as the bridge over the sonorously named Kilandan Blandan burn. Thereafter, bear left to the bridge over the Burn of Mar, which occupies a delightful site deep-set among rowan and birch: an idyllic lunch-spot for a warm day, especially with the 200 metre (700 feet) climb over Conic Hill in prospect. This little burn, like others along the Way, is the haunt of war-blers, dippers and wrens. The slope of Conic Hill rises beyond the top of the steep little rib above the bridge. The Way breaks off to rise steadily across the heathery banks of the hill. The gradual ascent, looking out over the bare moorland drained by the Burn of Mar, ends where the Way turns on to the north-west side of Conic Hill, to traverse its north face on a natural shelf beneath the humpback ridgecrest.

It is well worthwhile climbing up to the top of Conic – start from the point where the Way begins to drop westwards – to enjoy one of the widest and most varied panoramas of the whole West Highland Way. The hill itself is a fairly steep-sided hogsback ridge. It does appear conical from end-on, particularly from near Balmaha, but its name is less likely to come from its shape than from the Gaelic *A'Coinneach*, the moss or bog, which may be a transference from the moorland on its north and east. Conic Hill owes its distinctive character to the Highland Boundary Fault, and the trend of the fault is very obvious in the alignment of the islands in Loch Lomond.

But geology is rarely as simple as it seems: Conic is not a Highland rock formation raised by faulting above the Lowlands, but

Loch Lomond and its islands from Conic Hill.

the resistant edges of Lowland strata, warped to a high angle by the fault-line, which is actually to the north of the ridge. At several places on the top of the hill you can examine this rock, a chunky conglomerate of lower Old Red Sandstone age. It is full of varied and interesting fragments of older rocks, ranging in size from pebbles to boulders, cemented together by a dark red or almost purple sandstone; and on the descent towards Balmaha, you can readily observe, on looking back, how steeply inclined the beds of sandstone lie. On or close to the ridge-top there are also one or two foreign-looking erratic boulders of quite different formation, left behind by glacier ice as it overrode the ridge.

While much of the panorama from Conic Hill is a grander version of the southwards view from near Gartness or Garadhban, the added height gives it a new dimension. To the east, Ben Ledi near Callander appears as a flattened pyramid left of Gualann; to Gualann's right the distant Ochil plateau presents an abrupt scarp to the south, and in good visibility the Wallace Monument on Abbey Craig can be seen. The Gargunnock and Fintry Hills lead round to the familiar north front of the Campsies and to Strathblane. On the Kilpatrick hills the bun-shaped top of Duncolm, the highest point, is another old volcanic vent; to its right, through the gap of the Vale of Leven, the chimney of the Inverkip power station marks the Clyde. Beyond it the mountains of the Isle of Arran are a bonus in clear weather. In the foreground the Endrick meanders reluctantly into Loch Lomond. The marshes at its mouth, part of the Loch Lomond National Nature Reserve, are famous among bird-watchers for wildfowl and waders. But the *pièce de résistance* of the Conic view is Loch Lomond itself, which here for the first time presents its true character as a loch of both Highlands and Lowlands. Sir Walter Scott epitomised this aspect in Rob Roy:

> This noble lake, boasting innumerable beautiful islands of every varying form and outline which fancy can frame – its northern extremity narrowing until it is lost among dusky and retreating mountains – while, gradually widening as it extends to the southward, it spreads its base around the indentures and promontories of a fair and fertile land, offers one of the most surprising, beautiful, and sublime spectacles in nature.

On a clear day, the Way-walker will enjoy an inviting prospect of the route ahead, passing from sight where Ben Lomond looks over the loch to the rugged peaks of the Arrochar Alps. From here onwards, the West Highland Way is continuously in mountain country.

The easiest descent from the top of Conic Hill is to retrace your steps to the Way and continue the westwards traverse. The route drops steeply into a little grassy corrie between two limbs of the ridge, then turns down through a gap to the south-east, descending by a stepped path on steep slopes which in summer are covered in deep bracken. At its foot a track leads westwards again under the hillslope to the forest edge, and down through mature plantations to emerge at the public car park in Balmaha. The Way crosses the car park, and comes out on to the B837 road at the head of Balmaha bay. In the winter months Balmaha is a quiet backwater, but in summer it is much busier, and the bay fills with a colourful multitude of small boats.

Although it is a small settlement, Balmaha is an old-established one. It appears as 'Balmacha' in Blaeu's *Atlas* of the mid-seventeenth century, and may be much older, since it is thought to owe its name to St Maha or Mahew, a companion of St Patrick, who may have been a missionary in this area. Near the farm of Moorpark, above the Garadhban woods, there is a St Maha's Well which was long reputed by local people to have healing powers.

Under the active promotion of woodland management by the Dukes of Montrose, Balmaha became the site of a small factory producing pyrolignous acid or 'wood vinegar', a crude acetic acid, by distillation from oak thinnings and trimmings. The acid was used in the textile bleaching and dyeing industry in the Vale of Leven and the Glasgow area. At its peak the factory used up to 700 tonnes of small wood each year, but it closed during the 1920s when large-scale industrial production of chemicals took over the market.

Today the main activity in Balmaha is catering for day visitors; there is a shop, pub and B&B accommodation. A reasonable bus service runs south via Drymen to Balloch and the Vale of Leven, but there is no scheduled service north to Rowardennan. You will also find here the National Park Visitor Centre, which has lots of helpful information and interesting displays about the park. It also has toilets. The centre is open daily 09.30-16.30 from April to October.

Boat trips on the loch are available, and if you have time to spare,

Inchcailloch on Loch Lomond.

The Tom Weir statue at Balmaha (Paul Saunders Photography).

a visit to Inchcailloch, the nearest of the islands, is recommended. Inchcailloch is part of the Loch Lomond National Nature Reserve and has an excellent nature trail which describes the geology and the natural and human history of the island. A very informative leaflet about the trail can be picked up at the Visitor Centre.

Down by the shore is a life-size statue of the much-loved writer, broadcaster and mountaineer Tom Weir, unveiled in December 2014 by Tom's widow Rhona (then aged 94) and the outdoor writers and broadcasters Cameron McNeish and Jimmie MacGregor. A seating area and viewplace has been created here too. Tom Weir was famous for his lifelong exploration of the Scottish hills and glens and for the unique way in which he communicated his deep feeling for, and knowledge of, Scotland to his TV, radio and book audiences. The statue is a fitting tribute to the man and will undoubtedly become a focal point for outdoor enthusiasts. There are further plans to develop the area and fundraising for this purpose is ongoing.

During the 1930s boats were among the many means by which outdoor enthusiasts contrived to squeeze a full day on the hills from a one-day weekend. Jock Nimlin, one of the most enterprising climbers of the time, has described how he and his companions would catch a late bus from Glasgow on a Saturday night to arrive at Balmaha about midnight:

> Sometimes we arranged for a rowing-boat to be ready at Balmaha jetty and, rowing with two pairs of oars in two-hour shifts, we would cover the 14 miles to Tarbet by 4am, snatch a few hours' sleep under the trees and walk to Arrochar for a fair day's climbing before facing the return trip . . . I can still recall the bliss of an off-shift when one curled up between the feet of the swinging oarsmen – took a last look at the swaying stars and drifted into sleep to the slap and gurgle of the water.

Loch Lomond

Loch Lomond is the largest body of inland water in Britain, covering over 70 square kilometres (27 square miles). It is one of the longest Scottish lochs, at 37 km (23 miles) and one of the deepest: south of Inversnaid the bed of the loch drops to a depth of 190 metres (623 feet), of which all but 8 metres (27 feet) lies below sea-level. By general consent it is also among the most beautiful of Scottish lochs. In July 2002, the Loch Lomond and Trossachs area was officially designated Scotland's first National Park, an accolade it fully deserves. This should bring an injection of extra money for the conservation of the area and enable genuinely co-ordinated management of recreation, agriculture, water use and economic activity, to the benefit of the area as a whole. The West Highland Way follows the eastern shore of the loch for about 30 km (19 miles), giving the walker a vivid appreciation of its changing character and noble scenery.

The accepted view of geomorphologists is that Loch Lomond probably did not exist prior to the Pleistocene glaciation. Its site was occupied by the high headwaters of three rivers flowing east, with the divides between them roughly on the lines of Ben Vorlich-Beinn a'Choin and Ben Reoch-Ben Lomond. During the Ice Age these watersheds were breached by one of the great glaciers radiating

Loch Lomond at dusk.

from the vast zone of ice accumulation on Rannoch Moor, and a deep north-south trench was excavated.

As a result of these processes, Loch Lomond is in two distinct sections. In its southern part, up to Ross Point, the loch is wide, relatively shallow, and studded with islands. North from Ross Point it is rarely more than 1,500 metres (a mile) wide, is enclosed between steeply sloping hillsides that continue down to great depths, and has only a few small islands. It is a loch of both Highland and Lowland, a contrast reflected in climate, vegetation, wildlife and human history. The relatively flat low ground of the southern end, with moderate rainfall, is good arable farmland. It gradually gives way northwards to pasture and woodland, including Scotland's largest remnant of oakwood, on the slopes above the loch, which in turn pass upwards and northwards into bare open moorland and mountain characterised by high rainfall, extreme exposure and thin soils.

The area surrounding the loch presents a remarkable botanical variety: a quarter of all known British flowering plants and ferns have been found in the Loch Lomond catchment. Similarly, the gamut from marshland to mountain-top habitats attracts a wide variety of bird species, further augmented by the loch's position at a crossroads of migration routes; some 220 species have been observed. There is a correspondingly wide range of mammals,

29

from shrews to red deer, fallow deer and feral goats, and even a notable diversity of types of fish. The loch holds not only the common Scottish game fish, salmon, sea-trout and brown trout, and a number of coarse fish such as perch and roach (and some monster pike), but also a curiosity called the powan (*Coregonus*). This fresh-water herring, found in only a few other locations in Britain, was probably isolated in Loch Lomond during sea-level changes after the last glaciation, and may now be the most common fish in the loch.

In terms of human history the Loch Lomond area has been both a corridor of movement and a zone of conflict. While the people of the low country at the foot of the loch were settled farmers on land rented from titled magnates, those inhabiting the rough terrain to the north were small clans of lawless cattle traders and reivers; the interaction of the two kept the region in a state of tension for centuries. Into the nineteenth century a considerable population occupied the shores of even the Highland section of the loch; but most of the people and settlements have gone, and it is now difficult even to envisage the clachans that are listed in contemporary accounts at frequent intervals along the loch shore.

As a result of its accessibility from the Lowlands, Loch Lomond attracted many early travellers who were particularly intrigued by persistent reports of a floating island on the loch. The tourist trade gathered momentum in the later eighteenth century and flourished throughout the nineteenth under the stimulus of the writings of Sir Walter Scott. The loch remains one of Scotland's major tourist attractions, and an immensely popular area for day visitors from all over Central Scotland. The two main Visitor Centres are Lomond Shores at Balloch (open all year) and the National Park Gateway Centre at Balmaha (open Easter–October).

Balmaha – Rowardennan
(11.75 km; 7.25 miles)

The line of the West Highland Way from Balmaha to the hotel at Rowardennan is never far from the shore of Loch Lomond, winding up and down hill, into bays and round promontories, through open woodlands and conifer plantations. If for any reason you lose the route, the minor road that parallels the Way acts as a safety 'handrail'. Great care should be exercised on the road, however; it is narrow and winding, with short steep hills and blind bends. This section of the Way should not be hurried over, for its constantly changing scenery demands appreciation. The oakwoods are particularly rich in natural history interest, and there are many little gravel beaches and miniature headlands that offer ideal lunch spots or just an excuse for a rest on a sunny day.

It should be mentioned, in case you are tempted by a hot spell, that Loch Lomond has an ugly reputation as a trap for unwary bathers, and has claimed the lives of even strong and experienced swimmers. The shores are in places deceptively steep-shelving and the deeper waters are always chill, however invitingly warm the shallows may be. The loch is also liable to sudden sharp squalls of wind, perhaps caused by local funneling effects in the glens that run down to the loch. In 1829 one of these squalls struck a rowing boat in which the composer Felix Mendelssohn and a companion were crossing the loch, and came very close to upsetting it.

From Balmaha the Way sets off along a path between road and loch round the head of the bay. Where the road turns steeply uphill through the Pass of Balmaha, the Way carries on along the road to the old pier for 100 metres or so before it, too, climbs

Boats at Balmaha.

31

steeply up to the right and back to the top of the hill, which goes by the curious name of Craigie Fort. This is also part of the Balmaha Millennium Forest Trail.

On the flat top you will again notice the rough Old Red Sandstone conglomerate that forms the ridge of Conic Hill and the line of islands from Inchcailloch to Inchmurrin. From this vantage point, formerly crowned by a cairn marking the official opening of the West Highland Way in 1980, you can gather a good impression of the character of the whole southern end of the loch. Above the wooded eastern shore, Ben Lomond provides a challenging waymark.

Offshore lies a representative selection of the loch's islands: some large, some tiny, some almost flat, others rugged and high. Practically all of them were inhabited in the past, since they offered a refuge or a stronghold with a slightly higher degree of security in troubled times. Inchcailloch, the nearest – it looks only a stone's throw offshore – is typical in this respect. It is believed to have been the site of a nunnery in the early Christian era. According to tradition, St Kentigerna, the mother of St Fillan who gave his name to Strath Fillan near Crianlarich, died on the island in 734AD. Later the church on Inchcailloch served what is now Buchanan parish; in its graveyard are buried several members of the wild clans MacFarlane and MacGregor, who controlled the lands around the upper part of Loch Lomond. The island was farmed until about 1770, when the Duke of Montrose ended the lease and allowed it to revert to woodland.

Because this southern part of the loch is so open and shallow, it has been known to partially freeze over in severe winters, and on occasion the usual mailboat run to the islands has been performed on foot. In the 'Great Frost' of 1895 the ice cover was so thick and extensive that over 30,000 people came to walk, skate and curl on the loch. By contrast, it is unknown for the loch to freeze over north of Rowardennan.

From Craigie Fort, the Way heads briefly along the hilltop towards Conic Hill before dropping sharply down the north side of the hill through pleasant open oakwoods to the shore. It keeps close to the shore around Arrochymore Point and to the car-park at Milarrochy. The exposures of rock at the edge of the loch are of considerable interest; contrary to expectations, beds of red

Tiny island in the shallow waters of the Loch.

sandstone outcrop here, north of the Highland Boundary Fault.
These are the Upper Old Red Sandstones, laid down across the
faultline and later down-faulted, so that they have been preserved
here while erosion has stripped them from the country south of
the fault, where they stood higher. As the Way turns into Milarrochy Bay (car park and toilets) it crosses the northern limb of the
Boundary Fault and passes into the major Highland formations,
the Dalradian schists and grits.

At the back of the bay the West Highland Way takes to the
road to avoid a Camping and Caravanning Club campsite on the
shore. From Milarrochy Cottage it runs on the right-hand verge
as far as the bridge on the Blair Burn. Here it enters the Queen
Elizabeth Forest Park, which stretches from Loch Lomond eastwards through the Trossachs and covers some 17,000 hectares
(42,000 acres). The greater part of the oakwood on the land has
been retained, and is now managed in consultation with Scottish Natural Heritage. The Way follows a pleasant path on the
west side of the road, but screened from it by trees. It crosses the
stream below Blair Cottage by its own little plank bridge, and
goes up to the edge of the plantations on Strathcashell Point.
The path changes direction several times, but is always well
marked. After 700 metres or so, the forest gives way to more

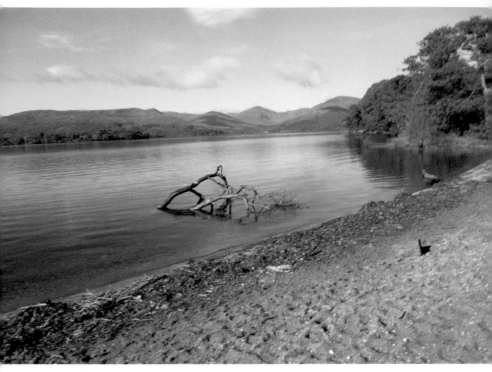

Milarrochy Bay.

open deciduous woodland. The route meanders gently down-hill to rejoin the road opposite the Cashel Farm road-end. The 'Cashel' of these place names is a complex of grassed-over dykes and ditches near the Point, thought by archaeologists to be an Iron Age fortification. Cashel Farm is now owned by the Royal Scottish Forestry Society. A major regeneration programme involving native trees is underway, and there are several good walks laid out.

The Way parallels the road on the long straight past the camp-site (with a useful shop) on the left, then clambers along a path on the verge and hillside as far as Anchorage Cottage. It is worth the effort to avoid the road, which is squeezed between loch and hillside with little room for traffic and pedestrians. The slight extra elevation allows glimpses of the island of Inchlonaig and the woods and meadows of Luss on the opposite shore. Inchlon-aig is notable for its yews, which tradition avers were planted on the instructions of Robert the Bruce to supply longbows for his archers, and for its fallow deer; the island was a private deer park of the Colquhouns of Luss from 1663.

At Anchorage Cottage the route takes the road again for a short distance to Sallochy, where it goes left towards the loch in fine open oakwoods. After a short stretch by the shore, it turns inland and climbs over a ridge to circumvent a steep rock rib that falls to the loch, barring passage by the shoreline. When the tree canopy is not too dense, this ridge gives an excellent view, with the abrupt narrowing of the loch at Ross Point standing in sharp contrast to the wide sweep of water and islands to the south. The route drops down to the north-west, returns to the shore, and continues close to it for about 800 metres through splendid oakwoods to the Sallochy campsite and car park by the bay.

The oakwoods that are Loch Lomond's crowning glory are no more than semi-natural. They are composed of both the standard British oaks, the sessile and the pedunculate, and many hybrids between them. This great hardwood resource was exploited in a remarkable range of ways from the fifteenth century on. At first, timber was cut for house-building and for the shipbuilding industry of Dumbarton. In the seventeenth century the oakwood provided the charcoal for ironsmelting in small local sites called 'bloomer-ies', until these were superseded in the later eighteenth century as iron production became concentrated in large-scale Lowland works using coal. Several bloomery sites have been identified up and down the loch's east shore by their characteristic mounds of purplish-black slag. You might come across a small site where bog ore was smelted almost anywhere below the tree line along the West Highland Way.

As the iron trade dwindled, the oak-bark industry which had complemented it came to the fore. The bark commanded a good price as a vital ingredient in the process of leather-tanning. Its production was based on a system of woodland management known as 'coppice-with-standards', in which the 'standard' tree was left to produce seed, while regenerating shoots were regularly thinned and the coppiced trees felled on a rotation of about 20 years. Thus in 1841 the Duke of Montrose ran a 25-year cycle on his 3,000 acres of oakwood, cutting 120 acres each year. The bark was exported by water to Glasgow, Ireland and the West of England.

THE WEST HIGHLAND WAY

Beyond the car-park the Way continues along the shore, passing between the Universities' Field Centre at Ross and its boathouse before striking steeply up into Ross Wood. Once on top of the hill, 73 metres (240 feet) above the loch, the route begins a long, gradual descent, giving glimpses ahead of Ben Lomond rising broad-shouldered over its wooded lower slopes. After about 600 metres, the Way approaches the edge of open pastureland, but then goes leftwards through the woods again to the cottage and outbuildings by the burn, close to the bay below Coille Mhor. This is a peaceful, secluded spot.

If the water-level in the loch is low, the remains of a crannog may be visible not far offshore in the bay. There are several of these lake dwellings in Loch Lomond; they fulfilled the same defensive role as the islands did, but were man-made structures created by dumping boulders, brushwood and timber into the shallows by the edge of the loch to form a large platform on which huts to hold men and beasts could then be constructed. A causeway of timber or stone, just below water level and hence invisible to hostile visitors, was built to link the crannog to the shore. The best-preserved of the Loch Lomond crannogs is off Strathcashell Point; most of them now show only a few protruding boulders. It is thought that they were built in the Iron Age, but in some parts of Scotland they continued in use up to the Middle Ages.

Beyond the stream the Way wanders along behind an alder swamp, crosses another burn, and climbs over a knoll in a hushed, needle-carpeted plantation of larch, from which it emerges at the inlet of Lochan Maoil Dhuinne. Beyond this inlet, the route continues on a good, undulating path through open oakwood which gradually thickens into a mixed plantation. Eventually, the Way turns inland and returns to the road just 300 metres south of the Rowardennan Hotel. You can find accommodation here, at the hotel and at the Youth Hostel some 750 metres further north, and transport: there are ferry links to Luss and Tarbet during the summer, and you may be able to get a boat (by prior arrangement with the Rowardennan Hotel) across to Inverbeg. There is however no bus service back to Balmaha.

Rowardennan is also the starting-point of the path up Ben Lomond, one of Scotland's most-climbed and best-loved peaks, and since 1982 in the ownership of the National Trust for Scot-

land. The Ben is not only an important milepost on the West
Highland Way, marking the first quarter of the route: it also has
the distinction of being, at 974 metres (3,195 feet), the most
southerly of Scotland's Munros – the 284 mountains over 3,000
feet (914 metres) listed originally by Sir Hugh Munro in 1891. By
inference, therefore, it should be an exceptionally good viewpoint,
and it is. In fair weather the ascent presents no difficulty, and can
be thoroughly recommended as a fine half-day walk. This area is
now known as the Ben Lomond Memorial Park (a park within a
park), and is dedicated to the memory of those who fell in the two
World Wars. There is a striking commemorative granite sculpture
set on a small point which commands a superb view up the loch,
just beyond the car-park.

The facilities here include the car-park, toilets and an interpretive display.

3
Rowardennan – Inverarnan

SUMMARY

Distance: 22.5 km (14 miles).

Height range: 20-100 m. **Total ascent**: 410 m.

Accommodation: Hotel and youth hostel at Rowardennan. Hotel and B&B at Inversnaid Hotel, B&B and campsite with wigwams at Inverarnan/Beinglas. Hotel, campsite and wigwam at Ardlui, accessible by 'on demand' ferry from Ardleish. The Loch Lomond WaterBus services can also be used to access other accommodation on the west bank of the loch.

Supplies: There are no shops directly on this section. Small shop at Ardlui Hotel.

Public transport: Seasonal water bus across Loch Lomond from Rowardennan and Inversnaid. Buses to Glasgow from Inverarnan. Trains to Glasgow from Ardlui (3 km from the route).

Terrain summary: This is perhaps the roughest section of the Way, particularly north of Inversnaid where the path along the side of Loch Lomond is slow going with many ups and downs. A full, hard day's walk but the scenery is superb.

Rowardennan – Inversnaid
(11.75 km; 7.25 miles)

From Rowardennan to the head of Loch Lomond the West Highland Way holds to the eastern shore of the loch: sometimes close by the water's edge, sometimes well up the slopes. The first section, to the hotel and road-end at Inversnaid, is a traverse through woodland under the steep flanks of Ben Lomond. Between Ptarmigan Lodge and Rowchoish bothy there is a choice between a low-level route, picking its way through the loch-shore oakwoods on a rough but scenic path, and a high-level

The loch shore towards Rowchoish.

route on the forest road, which gives easier and more straight-forward walking. These routes rejoin about 500 metres beyond Rowchoish; thereafter an excellent path winds gradually down to the loch-shore near Cailness and continues close above the loch by the wooded slopes of Craig Rostan to Inversnaid. In fine weather this is an idyllic walk through sun-dappled woods, with the loch glittering through the trees and a profusion of birdlife and bright, small flowers to add interest and colour.

A little way north of the Rowardennan Hotel, the public road ends at the large car park by the pier. There have long been pro-posals to push a road up the east shore of the loch at least as far as Inversnaid to complete a tourist circuit. This was strongly advocated by the minister of Buchanan parish in the *New Statistical Account of Scotland* in 1841, and proposed as relief work for the unemployed during the 1930s by Tom Johnston, later Secretary of State for Scotland. Happily, however, there is to date only the forest road to Rowchoish, and there seems little chance of that changing. If you

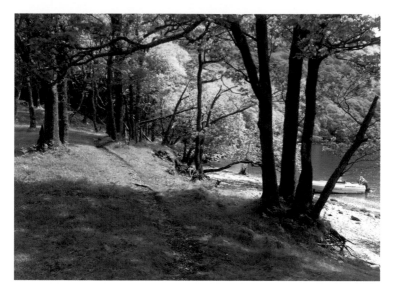

The forest route by the loch.

were dropping someone off at Rowardennan and picking them up at Inversnaid you would have to drive nearly 80 km (50 miles).

The Way follows the track up behind the car-park towards the Youth Hostel, but leaves it on the left and continues past the houses, NTS ranger base and bunkhouse at Ardess under the hill. There are remains of several iron-smelting bloomeries in this area, one of which can be seen on the Ardess Hidden History Trail. The Trail only takes an hour to complete and is well worth doing if you have the time. A descriptive leaflet is available. NTS have also built a replica of a traditional cruck-framed building at Ardess. A kilometre or so further on, the road forks, the left-hand branch being the drive to Ptarmigan Lodge; the Way goes right on the forest road, which now begins its gradual climb to over 200 metres (650 feet).

Ptarmigan Lodge takes its name from the spur of Ben Lomond above, which had that name as long ago as Roy's Map of about 1750. The ptarmigan may still be seen occasionally on the slopes of Ben Lomond, though usually off the path to the summit where there is less disturbance. A cousin of the red grouse, it will often let you come close enough to admire its handsome mottled plumage, which in winter turns snowy-white, before gliding off a short distance.

Some 300 metres beyond the Ptarmigan Lodge junction, the Way itself divides. The low-level route descends by a flight of steps to the shore; the upper route continues on the forest road, winding uphill through mixed plantations. The forest road provides easier and quicker walking, but it lacks much detailed interest and the outward views are generally restricted, though at the high point of the road, a memorial seat (to Tom Wheldon) offers a splendid view across the loch. *Note: At the time of preparing this edition, the lower route was closed due to storm damage.*

You will find in this area notices regarding camping restrictions. Unregulated camping (generally not by walkers) leading to litter and disturbance has been a serious problem along Loch Lomond, and the National Park felt it had to introduce some regulation in order to try to maintain the quiet and peaceful nature of the area.

The loch-shore route, through woodland of oak and birch, is distinctly rough in places; the going may be steep above the loch, or scrambling by the water's edge among boulders and broken crags. However, there are no very fearsome obstacles to overcome, and there are many compensations by way of wildlife interest and human history. One of the bigger crags, about 2.5 km (1.5 miles) beyond Ptarmigan Lodge, goes by the name of Rob Roy's Prison; here, it is said, he kept hostages and kidnap victims in a natural rock cell close above the loch. As with Rob Roy's Cave, north of Inversnaid, there must be some doubt as to whether Rob Roy ever used his 'prison', but this is certainly the beginning of his country; the lands of Craig Rostan from about here to the head of the loch were his property. Indeed at the beginning of the eighteenth century, Rob Roy and his MacGregor kinsmen held most of the territory from Loch Lomond east to Strathyre, and from Aberfoyle north to Glen Dochart.

The history of the Clan Gregor in general, and of Rob Roy in particular, has been so much romanticised and coloured by Sir Walter Scott and other writers that it is often difficult to distinguish fact from fiction. In the thirteenth century the MacGregors occupied the lands of Glen Strae and Glen Orchy at the head of Loch Awe, but fell foul of the expansionist strategy of the Campbells, who were able to use legal means to dispossess the MacGregors and drive them eastwards. The clan's subsequent history is one of occupying disputed lands, oppressed by powerful neighbours, and surviving by their wits, force of arms, and a good deal of cattle-thieving over the Highland line, later formalised, as already mentioned, into an efficient system of blackmail.

The MacGregors seem to have had an unhappy knack of backing the wrong side in a conflict, or attacking the wrong neighbours, a talent exploited by their enemies. At the beginning of the reign of Mary, Queen of Scots they took part in an abortive rebellion, and 'letters of fire and sword' were issued against the clan. In 1603 they massacred the Colquhouns in the Battle of Glen Fruin on the west side of Loch Lomond, and these letters were renewed and the name of MacGregor proscribed, the use of the surname being forbidden on pain of death.

This history explains much of the character and lifestyle of Rob Roy. The by-name Roy, from the Gaelic *ruadh*, he owed to his red hair. He was born in 1671 into one of the cadet families of the MacGregor chiefs, and by the time he was 30 he had shown his mettle by leading raids into the Lowlands, including the notorious Her'ship of Kippen, in which he carried off large numbers of cattle. He had married Mary, daughter of Gregor of Comer, under the north-eastern flanks of Ben Lomond; he had gained by gift or purchase the lands of Inversnaid and Craig Rostan; and he was established as a large-scale cattle dealer and drover.

The more lawless part of Rob Roy's career began in 1711, when his droving business collapsed after his head drover absconded with all the cash for the spring purchase of cattle; two of his chief debtors fled at the same time. The Duke of Montrose, Rob Roy's main creditor and for long an ally and confederate, had him first bankrupted and then outlawed; his house at Craig Rostan was burnt and his wife and family evicted. Rob Roy took to the hills, and began a long campaign of reiving against Montrose. In 1716 he captured his factor and carried him off – some say to the Prison. Unfortunately the Duke was reluctant to ransom his servant, and he was eventually released, minus the rents he had collected.

In later years Rob Roy seems to have led a more settled life, and died in his bed at Inverlochlarig, west of Balquhidder, in 1734. Two of his sons carried forward his less reputable activities till 1750, when they overstepped the mark by abducting a supposedly rich widow from Balfron and forcibly marrying her to one of their own number, Robin Oig. The brothers were pursued and broken, and the hanging of Robin Oig in 1754 marked the effective end of the MacGregors' wild career.

From the vicinity of the Prison northwards, there are superb views west through the Arrochar-Tarbet gap to the hills above Loch Long. The *pièce de résistance* in these views is the Cobbler, otherwise known as Ben Arthur; its craggy triple peaks make it a favourite haunt of Glasgow climbers. The pass between Loch Long and Loch Lomond, probably cut during the last Ice Age by a branch of the Loch Lomond glacier, is only a little over 30 metres (100 feet) above sea level, and may have been used in centuries past as a regular portage for small boats. The Gaelic name Tarbet implies a 'boatdrag', but by association it has come to be applied to any isthmus. This was certainly the route taken by Viking raiders in 1263, when forces under King Haakon were massed in the Clyde to assert Viking authority over western Scotland and the Hebrides. Haakon was eventually thwarted at the Battle of Largs, but not before a raiding squadron of perhaps 40 longships had been dragged over from Loch Long to Loch Lomond, where they wrought havoc along the Lennox shore and on the islands, pillaging and burning.

Beyond the Prison, the lower route continues along the loch and then leads uphill through conifers by a miniature glen to

Loch Lomond by Rowchoish.

Rowchoish. The bothy is almost invisible among the trees until you are within a few metres of it. It was restored to provide a basic shelter by the Forestry Commission and the Scottish Rights of Way Society as a memorial to William Ferris, a dynamic outdoor enthusiast from Glasgow. From the 1920s to his death in 1963, Willie Ferris was enormously active in outdoor organisations. Among much else he was a founder of the Rucksack Club from which the SYHA evolved; he founded the Scottish Ramblers Federation; and he was a director and chairman of the Rights of Way Society. As he was a great devotee of Loch Lomond, the bothy is a very apt memorial for him.

The remains of stone walls around the bothy are mute testimony to depopulation. There were nine families at Rowchoish in 1759, and at least three more settlements between here and Inversnaid, on a stretch of the shore where there is now only one cottage.

In good weather Rowchoish is an ideal place for rest and reflection. The view across the loch to the 'Arrochar Alps' is inspiring; the view north up the loch is inviting and stimulating. There is a glimpse of Inversnaid on the wooded east shore, and a distant prospect of the next mountain milepost, Beinn Dubhchraig, which appears as a flattened pyramid beyond the head of the loch. Since Beinn Dubhchraig and its neighbours, Beinn Oss and Beinn Lui, stand near the mid-point of the West Highland Way, and are high enough to be seen from a considerable distance, they are a particularly useful gauge of progress.

From Rowchoish the low-level route climbs gently through damp woodlands to rejoin the upper route on the forest road, only to have the road dwindle away after a few hundred metres. It gives way to a delightful path that winds through pleasant woods of birch, oak and pine for a while before descending to the northern boundary of the Forest Park, close by the loch-shore at the Cailness Burn. On the other side of the burn, under the hill, the trim farm cottage of Cailness commands a royal vista over open pastures to the loch and the mountains of the opposite shore.

The Cailness Burn has something of a turbulent recent history, with footbridges having been washed away twice: first in 1975 and again in 1985. The 1975 flood is commemorated by a cairn erected by members of staff from Cardonald College, Glasgow, whose colleague Bill Lobban lost his life trying to save one of a

Cailness Cottage.

party of students involved in a field exercise. The accident happened on 23 November 1975, when the group were crossing the burn and a member of the party slipped. Bill managed to save the student but in doing so was swept into the loch.

The West Highland Way carries on along the loch-shore as a well-marked trail. Generally it gives easy walking, though it does have a number of small climbs and there are several unbridged burns which could prove tricky if in spate. A notice welcomes you to Craigrostan Woods and explains the important work being done here to sustain and enhance the Atlantic oakwoods. This wooded stretch of lochside is very popular with birdwatchers. A few of the birds are conspicuous by their size and bright colouring, like the jay and the green woodpecker, both of which are here close to the northern limit of their breeding range. Some announce themselves by their call, like the cuckoo, or like the great spotted

45

woodpecker, by its drumming on trees. Many, however, are small and rather shy, such as the tiny treecreeper, which may be seen scurrying furtively up the trunks of oaks, picking at insects in the bark. It is worth sitting quietly for five or ten minutes simply to see what will appear.

The path arrives almost unexpectedly at Inversnaid, crossing the Snaid Burn just above its celebrated waterfall and descending to the car-park, pier and large Victorian hotel. The summer bustle of Inversnaid comes as an odd intermission in the Way's progress up the east shore of Loch Lomond. It occurs as a result of the one low break in the hills of the east shore: the road from Aberfoyle comes through a pass at only 150 metres (500 feet) by Loch Arklet. Geologists have suggested that this remarkable break is a remnant of the pre-glacial drainage patterns, when a river rising in the Arrochar hills flowed east across the present line of Loch Lomond, eventually to join the Forth. As evidence for their theory they point out the close alignment of the Inveruglas Water with the Arklet valley, and the 'hanging valley' character of the Snaid burn, with its steep-sided glen and waterfalls, suggesting that its direction of flow may have been reversed as a result of glacial erosion.

It was to cover this low pass, and thus to keep in check the activities of the MacGregors, that the Garrison of Inversnaid was built in 1718-19. The MacGregors did not take kindly to this intrusion on their lands, as they saw it. One night in August 1718 they kidnapped eight masons and quarriers from the site of the barracks and carried them off to the Lowlands before releasing them. Nevertheless the work reached completion in the following year, and the barracks were actively garrisoned until they were seized by the MacGregors during the 1745 Jacobite Rising. The site of the barracks can be seen a kilometre or so up the road towards Loch Arklet, though most of the stonework is incorporated into the buildings of Garrison Farm.

In the summer, WaterBus services run across the loch several times a day to Tarbet on the west shore. Because of its salient position, particularly for the nineteenth-century tourist traffic through Loch Lomond and the Trossachs, Inversnaid has a plethora of literary associations. The Wordsworths and Coleridge came here more than once in the course of their adventurous Highland

A WaterBus ready to depart.

tour of 1803; at the Inversnaid ferry-house they encountered the 'sweet Highland girl' lauded in one of Wordsworth's less successful poems.

Nearly 80 years later the Jesuit poet Gerard Manley Hopkins, with a sensitive vision sharpened, perhaps, by his missionary work in a squalid area of Glasgow, caught the spirit of the Inversnaid burn and wove it into a plea on behalf of wild nature:

> This darksome burn, horseback brown,
> His rollrock highroad roaring down,
> In coop and in comb the fleece of his foam
> Flutes and low to the lake falls home . . .
>
> What would the world be, once bereft
> Of wet and of wildness? Let them be left,
> O let them be left, wildness and wet;
> Long live the weeds and the wilderness yet.

Inversnaid – Inverarnan
(10.5 km; 6.5 miles)

THE section of the Way from Inversnaid to the foot of Glen Falloch is not only the roughest part of the whole route, it is also one of the finest. The east shore of Loch Lomond falls in a steep, broken, thickly wooded slope to the loch, which here lies deep and narrow where the glaciers have gouged out the valley bottom to over 150 metres below sea level. From Rob Roy's Cave north for about 3 km, much of the Way crosses wooded slopes close above the water's edge, with a good deal of up-and-down work: you should allow plenty of time for this stretch. A great deal of improvement work has been carried out, difficult sections have been smoothed over, and the path is now much easier than it once was, but one or two places still call for care, particularly with a pack on or in wet weather. Good boots are essential for this section. The difficulties, such as they are, end where the Way leaves the loch-shore about a kilometre south of Doune.

Inversnaid from the Loch.

Because this area is so rugged, it is relatively little visited and has a particularly rich flora and fauna. There are wild goats hereabouts, and even if you do not see them you may catch a whiff of their distinct musty odour. There is a special piquancy in the isolation of this part of the Way, sharpened by the hum of traffic on the A82 on the other side of the loch – at some points only a few hundred metres away, but in another world of human activity.

The footpath north from Inversnaid (now part of an RSPB reserve) is well-worn and often busy at first. Before reaching Rob Roy's Cave you encounter the first rocky section with some scrambling to be done. As compensation, you can enjoy superb tree-framed views across the loch to the Arrochar hills and the wooded slopes behind Inveruglas. Nathaniel Hawthorne, the American author, came here in 1857 and was firmly of the opinion that 'this particular stretch of Loch Lomond in front of Inversnaid, is the most beautiful lake and mountain view that I have ever seen'.

The scene has been changed somewhat since Hawthorne's visit by the creation of the Loch Sloy hydroelectric scheme, which has the largest generating capacity of all Scotland's conventional hydro schemes. The head of water is 274 metres (900 feet) and the catchment area was substantially enlarged by tunnelling and diversion works. Way-walkers might prefer not to know that Loch Sloy holds the Scottish record for maximum rainfall in 24 hours – 238.4 mm (9.39 inches) on 17 January 1974. The dam itself is hidden behind Ben Vorlich, but the downfall pipes running down to the power station at Inveruglas are conspicuous on the hill-front. 'Loch Sloy' was the watchword and battle-cry of the Clan MacFarlane who occupied the west shore of the loch north of Tarbet, and who had a castle on the small wooded island in Inveruglas bay. Like their MacGregor neighbours, the MacFarlanes had a fearsome reputation as raiders and cattle thieves.

Rob Roy's 'Cave' is not a cave at all in the strict sense, being more a deep crevice in the mass of enormous fallen blocks under Sroin Uaidh. There are signposts, but you may still have some difficulty finding it, as there are quite a few crannies and corners in the chaos of rock, and you should take care of your footing, particularly in wet conditions, when mica-schist can become as slippy as ice. Once you find the right crevice there is no mistaking

Loch Lomond near Inversnaid.

it, as a well-meaning enthusiast has daubed 'CAVE' in large white letters over the right-hand wall.

Given Rob Roy's association with this area, and the fact that his house was burnt by his enemies on more than one occasion, it is quite possible that he may have sheltered here. In earlier days, it was known as King Robert's Cave, in the belief that Bruce had used it in 1306 while a fugitive after his successive defeats at Methven and Dalrigh. There must, however, be a suspicion that both associations flow from the same romantic springs that have cluttered the Western Highlands with a surfeit of nooks called 'Bonnie Prince Charlie's Cave'.

The whole of the Loch Lomond area acquired an exalted romantic stature from the novels and poetry of Sir Walter Scott. His impact is epitomised in Dorothy Wordsworth's two visits to the cave: in 1803 she came with her brother and Coleridge; in 1822, four years after the publication of Scott's *Rob Roy*, she was accompanied by a large party from the loch steamer. A piper, a token Ancient Highlander, and boys selling bags of nuts were in attendance. Her fellow-tourists rushed to enter the cave, emerging to declare 'Well! there is nothing to be seen; but it is worth while, if only to say that one has been there!'

Beyond Rob Roy's Cave there is a straightforward path section for about 500 metres, but after that the sense of wildness quickly closes around the Way again. The path clambers up and down from the lochshore gravel to boggy flats, through high bracken and oakwood, under crags and fallen trees. This country is not much visited and is little grazed by animals. It displays a fascinating range of woodland and bog flowers, and a wide variety of woodland birds. As counter to the foreground detail there are views over the loch to the steep, bluff slopes of Ben Vorlich, shaggy with birchwood, and glimpses ahead to the next two mountain mileposts, Beinn Oss and Beinn Dubhchraig, gradually drawing nearer over the head of the loch on its western side.

As elsewhere in Scotland, the wilderness quality of this area is more apparent than real. Under Creag an Fhithich you will find the remains of the croft of Pollochro, now marked by three great sycamores and a rickle of stones on a boggy flat, but listed as an inhabited house in the seventeenth century and occupied within the century past. As you approach the Allt Rostan, the little, densely-wooded island called 'Island I Vow' will catch your attention. The curious name is a hopeless corruption of a Gaelic name – a previous anglicisation was 'Ylenow'. There is a ruin on the island, thought variously to have been a nunnery, a castle of the MacFarlanes, and a private house. Such is the history of Loch Lomond that it may well have been all of these at different times.

A short distance beyond the Allt Rostan the Way crosses a precipitous waterfall slab by a bridge perched virtually above the waters of the loch; the steps either side of the bridge are steep, and require a little care. A few hundred metres more of walking on the wooded slope, and the Way emerges on to the open gravel shore by the bay south of Doune – a pleasant and sunny spot for lunch or a break. The going from here on is more straightforward. The Way crosses the little stream that enters the bay and continues through the wood over the low hill to Doune. The network of dykes and the larch plantation on the hilltop convey a pleasant sense of domesticity contrasting with the rough country that the Way has come through. Doune Farm, long derelict, has been restored, while the outbuilding east of the house has been reconstructed by the Mountain Bothies Association as a bothy for Way-walkers and other outdoor folk – a welcome haven in a superb situation, looking north to the head of the loch.

The Way returns to the lochshore as it continues towards Ardleish, but the slopes are gentle and the walking easy. Below Ardleish it may be possible to summon and hire a ferry-boat from Ardlui for any walkers who feel their efforts on the Way have earned them a short trip to the facilities available across the loch. A noticeboard gives details. The Way continues uphill, passing above Ardleish; it crosses the burn and climbs on a path, which has largely been stone-pitched, to reach the marshy col at its head, where it continues to pass the eastern shore of the reedy Dubh Lochan.

The crest of the col is a superlative viewpoint, and effectively marks the end of the Loch Lomond section of the West Highland Way. Behind, the loch twists southwards between wooded promontories, with Ben Lomond a sharp cone peering over the craggy ridge of Craig Rostan. To the north the trinity of milepost mountains is completed as Beinn Lui appears to join Beinn Oss and Beinn Dubhchraig: all three now look comparatively close, soaring over the moors above Glen Falloch. Beyond the secret little valley of the Dubh Lochan, the path holds its height for a few hundred metres on a grassy shelf dotted with the broken walls of a ruined clachan, before running downhill to the foot of Glen Falloch. The glen in its lower part is a deep-cut, flat-floored glacial trench; its tributary glens are good examples of 'hanging valleys', and after rain the waterfalls on the western flank are a fine spectacle.

The path descends gently, winding through woods, to emerge on the flats a short distance south of the Ben Glas Burn. On this section you cross numerous small unbridged burns, but most are provided with good stepping-stones and should not present any difficulty unless conditions are exceptionally wet. A curious feature that you may notice as you descend is the Inverarnan canal, a short channel dug about 1850 to allow pleasure craft on Loch Lomond to bring their passengers right up to the Inverarnan hotel. Overhead, the transmission lines carrying power to and from the big pumped-storage hydro scheme of Cruachan, near Loch Awe, swoop across the valley.

This section ends at the bridge on the Ben Glas Burn, just before the wigwams, campsite and restaurant at Beinglas farm. Above the bridge the burn plunges nearly 300 metres in a kilo-

metre over a series of fine falls which can be awesome in wet
weather. Unfortunately the best of the falls cannot be seen from
the Way, as it is too close under the hill; to appreciate their full
height you must follow the short access branch of the Way leading round by the burn to the bridge over the Falloch, and so to
the A82 main road.

Over on the main road stands the hotel at Inverarnan, an ancient cattle-drovers' inn (built in 1705) on the route from Argyll
and the West round the head of Loch Lomond to the Lowland
markets at Crieff or Falkirk. The cattle were driven over the hills
from Glen Fyne – you will see the 'lairig' names signifying a pass
on the map – and then up the Ben Glas Burn into the Balquhidder or Glen Gyle valleys. In the nineteenth century, like many of
its counterparts, the inn became a tourist hotel and the canal link
with Loch Lomond was made. Nathaniel Hawthorne also came
to Inverarnan in 1857, and encountered the kind of weather that
is all too common in the Highlands: 'these clouds came down
and enveloped us in a drizzle, or rather a shower, of such minute
drops that they had not weight enough to fall. This, I suppose,
was a genuine Scotch mist; and as such it is well enough to have
experienced it, though I would willingly never see it again.'

From the 1880s the Inverarnan Hotel became a well-known
centre for climbers, and its hospitality was almost legendary.
During the 1930s it was a favourite base of the Glasgow section
of the Junior Mountaineering Club of Scotland. The author and
mountaineer W. H. Murray tells a tale of how he and two companions, having abandoned a January trip to Glen Coe in appalling
weather, made a nefarious entry to the hotel in the small hours of
the morning by forcing a window. They found a bed big enough
for three – 'the bridal suite, no doubt' – and slept undisturbed
till noon. He does not relate what the proprietors said when they
heard of the exploits of these midwinter 'honeymooners'.

Three kilometres (1.9 miles) further south on the A82 road
Ardlui offers a hotel, campsite, and shop, as well as railway and
bus services both northwards and southwards. Ben Vorlich is a
straightforward climb from near the hotel, and gives an excellent
retrospective view of this section of the West Highland Way.

4
Inverarnan – Crianlarich

SUMMARY

Distance: 10.5 km (6.5 miles).

Height range: 40-200 m. **Total ascent:** 365 m.

Accommodation: Hotel at Inverarnan. Campsite and wigwams at Beinglas Farm. Hotels, guest houses and B&Bs in Crianlarich.

Supplies: Small supermarket in Crianlarich.

Public transport: Regular buses and trains to Glasgow from Crianlarich.

Terrain summary: This is a short, pleasant section through Glen Falloch on good paths. The Way bypasses Crianlarich to the west but a spur path leads into the village, the halfway point on the route.

Breadalbane

FROM the head of Loch Lomond the West Highland Way continues northwards by Glen Falloch, Strath Fillan and upper Glen Orchy to the southern edge of Rannoch Moor. Between these valleys, the Way crosses and re-crosses the main east-west watershed of the Highlands. It is therefore appropriate to call this chapter Breadalbane, for this title, another historic division of Scotland, is generally taken to be a compound of *bra-ghad*, the Gaelic for an 'upper part', or the higher part of a slope, and Alban, the ancient name for Scotland, and hence means the upland of Scotland.

Glen Orchy and Glen Falloch both had vital links with the Earldom of Breadalbane, a powerful force in Scotland's history. Indeed, the family line of the Earls first sprang from the Campbells of Glenorchy, who gradually, by fair means and foul, extended their lands and power at the expense of neighbouring clans like the MacGregors till they achieved the Earldom in 1677. The first Earl was particularly notorious for his devious self-seeking, and was

Glen Falloch.

implicated in the Massacre of Glen Coe. One of his contemporaries described him as being 'cunning as a fox, wise as a serpent, but as slippery as an eel'.

As part of their 'empire building', the Campbells bought the estate of Glenfalloch in 1599. A cadet branch of the family held the land and style of Glenfalloch till 1867, when on the demise of the senior lines of succession, William Campbell of Glenfalloch became sixth Earl of Breadalbane. Under his son, the third Marquis, the Breadalbane estates reached their greatest extent, stretching in a great belt from Aberfeldy to the west coast islands of Luing and Seil and totalling over 160,000 hectares (400,000 acres). In his comprehensive study *In Famed Breadalbane* the Rev. William Gillies quotes a pithy verse about these vast landholdings:

> From Kenmore to Ben Mohr
> The land is a' the Markiss's;
> The mossy howes, the heathery knowes,
> An' ilka bonnie park is his.
> The bearded goats, the toozie stots,
> An' a' the braxy carcasses;
> Ilk crofter's rent, ilk tinker's tent,
> An' ilka collie's bark is his.

> The muircock's craw, the piper's blaw,
> The gillie's hard day's wark is his;
> From Kenmore to Ben Mohr,
> The warld is a' the Markiss's!

After the death of the Marquis in 1922, however, death duties caused the dismemberment of these great estates: Glen Falloch and Glen Orchy have passed into other hands.

Much of Breadalbane is deer and sheep country, with cattle-rearing on the valley floors, but in recent years there has been considerable afforestation, largely by the Forestry Commission. The natural history of the country evolves with the woodland; as the ground is ploughed and planted, the birds of grassland and heather moor, the lark and the pipit, the curlew, plover and grouse, give way to willow-warblers, finches and tits. Fencing to exclude sheep and deer allows grass to grow more thickly, encouraging mice and voles, which in turn enlarges the scope for predators on the ground, like stoats and weasels, and in the air, such as kestrels and short-eared owls.

In woodland or moorland the great scavenger is the 'hoodie', or hooded crow, readily identified by its grey back and underparts and its generally villainous demeanour; its breeding range extends as far south as the Highland edge, but it interbreeds with the common, carrion crow a good deal. Buzzards are not uncommon, and may be mistaken for the golden eagle until a genuine eagle appears, when the difference in size, shape, and flight becomes evident; but the chances of seeing eagles are not as good here as further north along the West Highland Way.

Inverarnan – Crianlarich
(10.5 km; 6.5 miles)

FROM the head of Loch Lomond the Way runs up Glen Falloch and over a low pass to Crianlarich in Strath Fillan. The River Falloch is the dominant element throughout; from Beinglas Farm the route follows the east side of the river for nearly 4.75 km to Derrydaroch, crosses it, and holds to its west bank for another kilometre before climbing to join the old military road above the A82 trunk road. The old road takes the Way on to Crianlarich and gives wide views of the open upper glen and the range of mountains among which the Falloch has its sources.

To join the West Highland Way from the Inverarnan Hotel, go north up the A82 road for a few hundred metres, cross the Falloch by the bridge over to Beinglas, and turn sharp right to follow the bank of the river and the Ben Glas Burn to the footbridge. From this bridge the Way goes along behind Beinglas Farm, following a farm track northwards. Almost from the outset there is a sense of enclosure in the valley bottom, with restricted views that are characteristic of the lower part of Glen Falloch. A little over a kilometre from the farm the mood changes. The glen now runs up towards the north-east, with open moorland flanks. The river surges in wide, low falls over a rocky bar, and the Way starts its steady ascent out of the Loch Lomond basin.

From here on till the Way leaves it, the Falloch is a long and splendid succession of gorges, rocky rapids, short cascades, cauldrons and wide dark pools, with short stretches of smooth water between. In wet weather it can be an awesome sight, but beware of venturing too close on the slippery schists of the banks. Geologists suggest that this spectacular course is a product of the complex history of drainage diversion in the Loch Lomond basin during and after the Pleistocene Ice Age. According to one theory,

Glen Falloch moorland.

the Falloch and all its tributaries north from the Ardlui area previously drained north-eastwards to join the River Fillan, and thence the Tay, in the vicinity of present-day Crianlarich. Even after thousands of years, it seems that the river is still adjusting its course to a new line of flow. On its progress up the Falloch the Way constantly moves from birch, alder and oak woodland to open pasture, and back again. Among the trees the going can give a sense of wildness entirely at variance with the occasional glimpses of traffic on the road or railway only a short distance away.

There was an odd little skirmish in Glen Falloch in November 1845. At that time, during the height of the great railway mania that swept Britain, several proposals were mooted for routes through this area. The Duke of Montrose, a director of the proposed Caledonian Northern Direct line, sent a survey party into Glen Falloch, the property of the Marquis of Breadalbane, himself a director of the rival Scottish Grand Junction. When news of the trespass reached Breadalbane country, a body of men, mostly miners from the lead mines at Tyndrum, came down the glen, overwhelmed the CND party, and threw them and their theodolite into the ditch. In the event, their efforts proved superfluous, as the mania burned itself out shortly afterwards; it was another 45 years before the West Highland line was built through the glen.

On the open stretches, particularly opposite the Fionn Ghleann, you may catch a glimpse of one or all of the three big milepost Munros to the northwest: Beinn Dubhchraig, Beinn Oss and Beinn Lui. These give a fine long hill-walk, but are better taken from the Strath Fillan side. From the same area you should look for the great boulder called Clach-na-Briton, 'the stone of the Britons', on the slope of Cruachan Cruinn above the glen. This huge rock is supposed to have marked the boundary between the territories of the Britons, the Scots and the Picts during the Dark Ages.

The path continues to Derrydaroch. The name means 'the oak grove', and there are some oaks by the river, though pines are increasingly the dominant tree in the upper parts of the glen. These pines, scattered along the lower slopes of the valley sides, are a remnant of the old Wood of Caledon, the great pine forest that clothed the central part of the Highlands in the post-glacial period. Burning, grazing and felling for timber,

Spring bluebells in the pine woods.

perhaps in conjunction with climatic changes inhibiting natural regeneration, have gradually reduced the forest to the present widely dispersed fragments. Two larger remnant woods can be seen near the Way a little further north. These pine woods were the original habitat of the native red squirrel; you are more likely to see it here than on Loch Lomondside, where the introduced grey squirrel has effectively taken over the deciduous woods. This section of woodland is fenced off and under active management to encourage regeneration.

The Way crosses the Falloch at the Derrydaroch bridge and turns sharp right over a birchwood knoll to return to the riverside. About a kilometre north from the bridge, the route climbs from the river to pass under the railway by a low-roofed cattle creep – an awkward passage if you are carrying a big pack. It passes under the A82 road by a tunnel, a short distance north of Carmyle Cottage, and strikes directly uphill for about 100 metres to join the old military road running under the electricity transmission line. The old road, an obvious grassy pathway, continues northwards along the hillside, and leads the Way the rest of the distance to Crianlarich.

The system of military roads in Highland Scotland was created largely in response to the Jacobite risings of 1715 and 1745. In the first great burst of activity, about 400 km were built under the command of Major General George Wade, who first identified the need for improved communications to pacify the area in his report on the state of the Highlands in 1724. During the ten years after 1725 Wade's main efforts were concentrated in the Central Highlands and Great Glen, linking the major Hanoverian forts and barracks in those areas.

It was left to Wade's successor as 'roadman', Major William Caulfeild, to fill out the skeleton of the road network. Between 1746 and 1767 Caulfeild directed the construction of over 1,300 km of roads in Scotland, including all the sections now used by the West Highland Way, although a good part of his work was outwith the Highlands, in the North-East and Galloway. Despite this, Wade tends to get the credit for all the roads; as the well-known couplet has it:

> If you had seen these roads before they were made,
> You would hold up your hands and bless General Wade.

The roads were military not only in purpose but also in construction; they were built largely by troops, who earned double pay for the work, with a few civilian masons to help with the bridgeworks. The techniques employed were basic: a road-bed was cut by excavation on flat ground or by benching on slopes; the spoil was heaped into banks on either side, and the paving was built up in layers of gravel, the material getting smaller in successive layers. Cross-drains were usually open and stone-lined; culverts were a later sophistication. All the materials used were local, causing the civilian population to complain that the roads tended to run between ready sources of gravel, rather than following the route most convenient to peaceful travellers.

The old road gives wide views over upper Glen Falloch to the Crianlarich hills. The south-western peaks are characterised by long spurs radiating from craggy, knobbly tops; but a little further north along the Way, Ben More begins to appear as a massive, steep pyramid beyond the ridges of Cruach Ardrain. At 1,174 metres the 'big ben' is the fifteenth highest mountain in Britain, and since its northern slope surges in one great sweep from the floor of Glen Dochart at about 170m to the summit, it shows its height to full advantage. In good conditions the

A distant view of the Crianlarich Hills.

view from the cairn is magnificent, and takes in much of the Central Highlands.

The Way continues above Keilator Farm, following the upper side of the dyke that encloses the improved ground. As a settlement Keilator pre-dates the military road; in a seventeenth-century manuscript the name is listed as 'Chuletyr', suggesting that it may mean 'the nook on the slope'. Beyond the house and farm buildings, dyke and Way together run into the head of a little glen and follow it upwards. This deep-cut miniature valley is probably a former glacial meltwater channel by which dammed-up water escaped from Strath Fillan into Glen Falloch, perhaps at a period when the lower col a little to the east, now occupied by the main road and railway, was choked by ice. It goes by the name of Bogle Glen, a bogle being a Scots ghost, ghoul or goblin, but tradition is silent on the origin of the name.

At the narrow head of the glen the Way passes from the Loch Lomond drainage system into that of the Tay, from the Atlantic side of Scotland to the North Sea side. This notable watershed is marked by a deer-fence and a gate protecting the Forestry Commission plantation to the north. Beyond the forest fence the route divides: the Way proper slants uphill leftwards to a knoll above a little crag, well worth visiting for its wide view up and down Strath Fillan with the fine company of mountains that stand over it. The

61

Glen Dochart from above Strath Fillan.

old military road continues as a little-used path heading north, down to the A82, 700 metres west of Crianlarich. Many walkers will, however, want to follow the spur path to the village to find accommodation, refreshments, supplies or transport.

The path winds gently down through mixed woodland, and near its foot is confronted with the new A82 Crianlarich bypass, opened in spring 2015. An airy underpass has been provided for walkers, but although the underpass has attractive stone walls acting as portals, the new sections of path to either side of the underpass are (at the time of writing) pretty rough. The surface is of coarse stones, quite unpleasant to walk on, and particularly above the underpass, the path is not well graded and should be stepped. Hopefully a better path can be provided before long.

The path divides near its foot. Going straight on and crossing the road (now much quieter) leads to the station and the village centre, with an excellent small supermarket/post office, and the youth hostel. Keeping left and following the road under the railway bridge (no footpath so take care) leads to the Crianlarich Hotel, which offers accommodation, a full range of meals, tea and coffee, and is always welcoming to walkers.

Crianlarich has the particular interest for Way-walkers of being roughly at the halfway point on the West Highland Way. The origin of its name is open to dispute though *craobh an lairig*—the tree by the pass—seems plausible. The historic origins of the settlement are uncertain too, since although Crianlarich now stands at the junction of both road and railway, it is already clear that the junction of the military road was some distance away; the site is a restricted one, between the morainic deposits on the pass and the ill-drained floodplain of Strath Fillan. In any event, Crianlarich owes much of its present character to its railway links and the subsequent tourist trade.

Crianlarich is still a centre of communications, with rail and bus services to Glasgow, Oban and Fort William. The village is equipped with shops, tearooms, post office and police station with a mountain rescue post. There is a reasonable range of accommodation, but remember it is a popular touring centre during the summer, and prior booking might be advisable at this time. The effects of the bypass on the economy of the village have yet to be revealed.

Because of its accessibility and the big hills around it, Crianlarich has long been a Mecca for hillwalkers. Many Scottish mountaineers who learned their hillcraft in this area hold its highly individual Munros in great affection. Anyone with time in hand can profitably spend two or three days here, since a dozen or more fine hills can be reached from Crianlarich in a summer day's walking. There is a good deal of broken crag on these hills, and they demand respect and route-finding skills, particularly in misty and wet conditions, but still more so in winter or spring when rocks may be ice-glazed and snow-slopes hard-frozen. The shoulder of Ben More facing Crianlarich and the steep north-eastern aspect of Cruach Ardrain are notoriously dangerous in winter. In those conditions ice-axe and crampons, and skill in their use, are vital: and this is true of most of the bigger hills from here on northwards.

5
Crianlarich – Bridge of Orchy

SUMMARY

Distance: 21.5 km (13 miles).

Height range: 120-330 m. **Total ascent:** 430 m.

Accommodation: Hotels, guest houses and B&Bs in Crianlarich and Tyndrum. Youth hostel in Crianlarich. Campsite at Tyndrum. Hotel at Bridge of Orchy. Wigwams at Auchtertyre.

Supplies: Small supermarket in Crianlarich. General store in Tyndrum.

Public transport: Regular trains and buses to Glasgow and Fort William from Crianlarich, Tyndrum and Bridge of Orchy.

Terrain summary: This section is on generally good paths and tracks with some moderate ascent and descent, but nothing unduly difficult and nowhere far from services. A straightforward day of glen and low pass walking amid outstanding mountain scenery.

Crianlarich – Tyndrum
(10.5 km; 6.5 miles)

IN its progress up Strath Fillan, the West Highland Way takes a pleasantly serendipitous course, first in the forest plantations on the southern slopes of the valley, then across the river and over farmland on its north side, and latterly by open moorland to Tyndrum. The strath has a particular charm in running among high mountains and moors, but retaining much of the atmosphere of a lowland valley.

From Crianlarich, the best way back onto the Way proper is to retrace your steps on the spur route, which starts at a waymarker and map in the small car-park across the road from the station. The Forestry Commission ploughing and planting in this area took place about the same time as the creation and marking of

The Way coming from Crianlarich.

the Way, so the opportunity was taken to integrate the route into the planting programme. A wide variety of species was planted, and breaks left at strategic points to provide maximum interest and amenity for walkers.

From the rocky knoll above the old military road the Way heads north-northwest, climbing gradually and commanding fine views back over Crianlarich to Ben More and Stob Binnein, and across the valley to Ben Challum. Where the slopes begin to run in towards the Herive Burn, the route turns north and descends into the valley, which in spring is richly clothed in primroses. It crosses the burn by a sturdy footbridge and then weaves a mazy way through the trees, with views across to the hills on the south of the glen. The Way drops down to the railway, passing an attractive waterfall, and then under a viaduct, follows the south side of the A82 road for a short distance before crossing it, then

65

sidles down a path below the road embankment and across a grassy meadow to the Kirkton bridge on the wide-flowing Fillan, a splendid viewpoint for the big Crianlarich hills; it then follows the farm road to Kirkton, and skirts the farm buildings on the left. The two farms on this side of the river are experimental units operated by the Scottish Agricultural College.

Among the trees by Kirkton Farm are the ruins of St Fillan's Chapel. An interpretive board tells something of the fascinating history of the man and his life. St Fillan was an Irish monk, the son of St Kentigern who, as mentioned earlier, died on Inchcailloch in Loch Lomond in 734AD: he was active as a missionary in Breadalbane, and many miraculous tales of his exemplary life and work have been handed down. It is uncertain whether Fillan himself had a chapel here, but the site appears to have been a monastic establishment around the twelfth century, and it was raised to a priory by Robert the Bruce in 1318. The reasons for Bruce's beneficence can only be guessed at; he may well have received spiritual or secular assistance from the monks at the time of his defeat at nearby Dalrigh in 1306. According to one old tale, St Fillan gave a miraculous sign of his support to Bruce on the eve of the Battle of Bannockburn. A relic of the saint, his arm-bone encased in silver, had been brought to the field as a talisman. As Bruce prayed before it, the case opened spontaneously to reveal the relic – to the astonishment of its priestly guardian, who (sensibly, in the circumstances) had brought only the case to Bannockburn, and had left the precious arm-bone in Strath Fillan for safety's sake.

The relics of St Fillan form perhaps the most remarkable part of the chapel's associations. Tradition relates that Fillan gave five symbols of his mission to lay brothers, who were required to act as custodians of the relics and to use them in appropriate circumstances, such as curing the sick or in the taking of oaths. These hereditary custodians, called in Gaelic *deoradh*, a stranger, anglicised as the surname Dewar, were given grants of land and special privileges which made them important dynasties in Glen Dochart and Strath Fillan; even the Reformation seems to have had little impact on their exalted status.

Only two of the relics are now known; the nature of the other three is a matter for speculation. The head of Fillan's crozier or staff, known as the Quigrich, travelled far with its keepers, and eventually went with them to Canada in 1818. It was recovered by the Society of Antiquaries of Scotland in 1877, and is now in the Museum of Scotland in Edinburgh. It is a superb piece of ornate silverwork, thought to be fourteenth-century, but was found to contain within it a much older crozier of a severely simple design. St Fillan's bell is also in the Museum of Scotland after a rather similar career. It was stolen from the chapel by an English visitor in 1798, and retrieved only in 1869, through the good offices of the Bishop of Brechin. The bell was kept at the chapel for use in a curious rite practised there as a supposed cure for insanity. Sufferers were dipped in a pool in the River Fillan known as the Holy Pool, carried to the chapel, and left overnight bound to a tombstone or the ancient font, with the bell over their head. In the morning it was expected that they would be found cured. The parish minister in 1843 took a wry view of these proceedings:

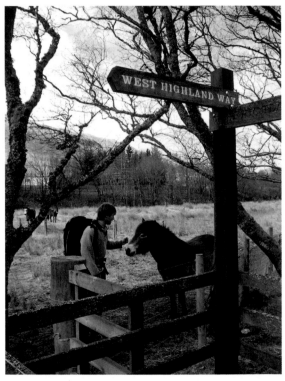

A change of direction along the Way.

> We have not heard of any being cured; but the prospect of
> the ceremony, especially in a cold winter evening, might
> be a good test for persons pretending insanity.

There are interpretive panels at the Chapel.

The Way follows the farm track along to the bridge at Auchtertyre Farm (which has no fewer than 18 wooden wigwams plus one alternative design called a yurt), and under a remarkable ridge of fluvio-glacial material back towards the river, which it reaches just above the Holy Pool. It crosses the A82 at the north end of the bridge across the Fillan and enters Tyndrum Community Woodland, occupying 90 hectares of hillocky land formed from glacial debris. The area was formerly planted with Sitka spruce by the Forestry Commission, but a fire destroyed most of the plantation in the early 1980s. About half of the area has regenerated or has been replanted using Caledonian pine and native broadleaves from local seed.

The Way continues along the river bank past the old White Bridge to the junction with the Crom Allt. A hundred metres or so up this burn, a rough track crosses it on a bridge; at the top of the hill beyond, the West Highland Way turns sharp right on a hard surfaced track which leads past a little lochan where a large stone marks the place where Robert the Bruce is said to have lost his sword and the brooch of Lorne into the water. The path leads to a terrace edge above the Crom Allt. This terrace provides the line of the Way through the regenerating woodland up to the mature pinewood below Tyndrum.

The whole area around the River Cononish above White Bridge is a jumble of hummocky sands and gravels, partly terraced by river action and representing the finer material deposited by meltwater in the later stages of the last glaciation. This area is known as Dalrigh (the King's field), commemorating a skirmish here in the summer of 1306 in which Robert the Bruce was defeated by the MacDougalls of Lorne, allies of his arch-enemies the Comyns. Dalrigh marked the low point of Bruce's fortunes; after he had been crowned King of Scotland at Scone in March, and defeated at Methven, near Perth, by an English force in June, he had taken to the hills with a small company of supporters, only to meet defeat once more.

The exact location of the battle is unknown, but John Barbour in his epic poem *The Brus*, written in the 1370s, described how the king fought off three attackers single-handed:

> . . . in ane narow place
> Betuix ane lochside and ane bra
> That was so strat, I undirta,
> That he micht nocht wele turn his sted

– a description which fits the little lochan which the Way passes on the terrace above the Crom Allt.

At the lower edge of the pinewood just below Tyndrum, a curious, barren patch of ground on the river bank is a reminder of a once thriving lead-mining industry. The Tyndrum lead vein was discovered in 1741 while the mineral rights of the Breadalbane estates were on lease to Sir Robert Clifton, after whom the miners' village was named. Up to 1745 he extracted nearly 1,700 tons of ore. Four successive companies then operated the mines till 1858, when the Marquis of Breadalbane resumed his rights and worked

A sheep-creep under the Oban railway line.

69

them till his death in 1862. Over that period another 5,000 tons of ore were mined, much of it yielding lead at nearly 50% of the ore weight, as well as small amounts of silver.

It was during the tenure of the Scots Mining Company from 1768 to 1790 that the crushing and smelting plant by the river was brought into operation; before then the crude ore was taken south by way of Loch Lomond at great expense. In its heyday the industry supported a population of around 200 in Clifton. In 1994, planning permission was given for gold to be extracted from a vein in Beinn Chuirn, north of Beinn Lui. After several delays, exploration of the vein has now started.

The Way follows the Crom Allt burn, passing below the site of the former goods yard by the station on the Oban railway line. It then goes through a wicket gate by the level crossing and across the gravel flats by the Crom Allt to the lower end of Clifton village, which is no more than a row of former miners' cottages. You will notice that the original axis of Clifton ran roughly south to north along the old road, but is now crossed at right angles by the main A82. There is a useful general store in the village – the last on the Way before Kinlochleven – as well as other shops, a restaurant and tearooms and hotel, bed and breakfast and bunkhouse accommodation, and a campsite. As at Crianlarich, there are bus and train services on all the routes through Tyndrum.

Tyndrum means simply 'the house on the ridge', the ridge in this case being the main east-west watershed of Scotland a short distance to the west. Perhaps because it stands far inland at the headwaters of the Tay, the inn at Tyndrum was long thought to be, as the *Old Statistical Account* put it in 1793, 'one of the highest inhabited situations in North Britain'. In fact it stands at around 230 metres, which is substantially lower than large settlements like Braemar or Wanlockhead.

Tyndrum was something of a service centre during the eighteenth and nineteenth centuries for the cattle droving trade, when the small black cattle of the Highlands were moved south 'on the hoof' to the markets or trysts at Crieff or Falkirk, where they were sold to Lowland or English dealers. Latterly there was a smithy where cattle could be shod – an unlikely but necessary measure when the beasts moved from the soft open ground of the upland drove routes to the enclosed gravel roads of the lower ground. There was a 'stance' where cattle and sheep could be rested overnight, and the inn, maintained by Lord Breadalbane, for the drovers themselves.

The intrepid Mrs Sarah Murray of Kensington put up at Tyndrum one wet autumn night in 1799 during her first tour in Scotland, just as the drovers were making their way home to the Highlands from Falkirk Tryst. As the evening wore on, the inn gradually filled to bursting point: 'this continued till the house was in a perfect uproar: my servants could not get a place to put their heads in. My man took his sleep in the carriage: and the poor horses were almost crushed to death in the stables'.

Things are not so very different in Tyndrum in high summer nowadays, when the village is full of the bustle and traffic of a busy tourist centre. In the winter or in wet weather, however, it can still be as Queen Victoria saw it when she passed through in 1875, 'a wild, picturesque and desolate spot'.

Tyndrum - Bridge of Orchy
(11 km; 6.75 miles)

FROM the upper end of Clifton village the Way climbs by the burnside towards the pass ahead in a purposeful manner which indicates that it is once more back on the line of the old military road. In fact, the Way makes use of the old road for much of the rest of its length, and diverges from it only slightly until within about 7 km of Fort William, when it breaks away to cross into Glen Nevis. Most of this distance gives excellent walking on a very clear track.

The first section, as far as Bridge of Orchy, is around 10km. This part of the Caulfeild road network was constructed by soldiers between 1750 and 1752 and was later adopted as the line of the old main road north through Glen Coe. The new road, built in the late 1920s and early 1930s, takes a sweeping curve westwards from Clifton past its junction with the Oban road, returning to join up with the old road and the railway as they enter the defile through to Glen Orchy. As it was built on a completely new line over much of its length, the new road is characterised by long, even curves and easy gradients. Although it is now taken very much for granted, at the time of its building amenity and recrea-

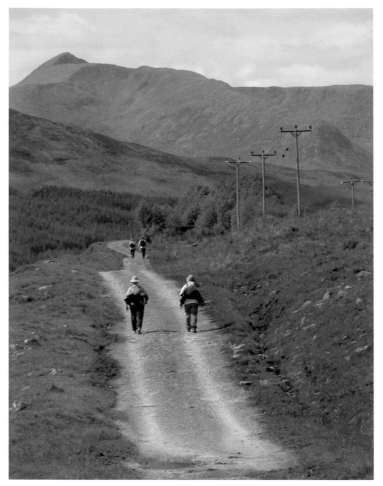

Heading from Tyndrum to Bridge of Orchy.

tion interests objected very strongly to its effect on the landscape, describing it as a 'million-pound racetrack'.

As the Way climbs there are fine views back across the head of Strath Fillan to the bulk of Beinn Dubhchraig and over the workings and debris of the lead mines on Sron nan Colan behind Clifton. The workings cover a very restricted area on a single main vein associated with an almost vertical fault line, which has been picked out by erosion. In fact, the quartz 'mother vein' continues northwards in the glen of the Crom Allt beside the Way, and it may be possible to detect the signs of excavation where unprofitable exploratory pits were dug around the stream. It is well worth examining the little gorge of the Crom Allt for its own sake, for it has one or two fine miniature cascades and 'punchbowls'; but the upper part of the glen is now dominated by the storage tanks and treatment plant of Tyndrum's water supply.

The steep-sided pass through to Glen Orchy is most probably another product of the last glacial epoch, when great glaciers flowed southwards from the major centre of ice accumulation on Rannoch Moor, and overrode the cols on ridges to the south. The slopes of Beinn Odhar on the right have been over-steepened in the process; the conspicuous scree-fans from the little burns on this flank, and the very clear terracettes or sheeptracks, testify to the slope's gradual adjustment under the force of gravity. It is not surprising that the soldiers building the military road spent much time and effort in this area clearing the road after rainstorms and spring thaws.

On the long, gradual ascent to the summit of the pass, Beinn Dubhchraig, a feature of the view from Rowchoish Bothy onwards, finally passes out of sight, just as the next of the great mountain mileposts of the West Highland Way, Beinn Dorain, soars into view ahead. With its bald, bouldery pate, sweeping slope to westward, and gully-seamed flanks, Dorain is a distinctive and challenging peak if not, perhaps, a very beautiful one. It dominates the Way as it passes the local authority boundary on the summit, leaving Stirling for Argyll and Bute, and also finally leaving the National Park. The path traverses above the east side of the railway line for 300 metres or so before descending sharply to go under the line to rejoin the old road. A little further down, the little schisty crags above the road are veritable hanging gardens of the yellow mountain saxifrage in summer.

The full, thousand-metre bulk of Beinn Dorain becomes ever more evident on the descent into Auch Gleann, where the wide horizontals of the open valley floor seem to sharpen the mountain's vertical contrast. The railway's remarkable horseshoe curve under the flanks of Beinn Odhar, Beinn a'Chaisteil and Beinn Dorain, and its viaducts over the intervening glens, lend further emphasis to the scale and steepness of the peaks.

Auch – the name is short for *Ach-innis-chalean*, the field of the hazel meadow – was once a royal hunting lodge. The Campbells of

Glenorchy, the hereditary keepers of the forest, and the forebears of the Earls of Breadalbane, were required to supply venison to the king; venison was even salted and exported to Spain.

The deer forests also served as inspiration for one of Gaeldom's greatest poets, Duncan Ban Macintyre, who was a stalker in Mamlorn. *Donnchadh Ban nan Oran* (fair-haired Duncan the poet – literally 'of the songs') was born near Loch Tulla in 1724, and although the details of his life are uncertain, he is believed to have lived for several years at Ais-an t-Sithein in Gleann Chonoghlais behind Beinn Dorain. He was called out in the Argyll Militia on the Hanoverian side, and participated very briefly in the Battle of Falkirk in January 1746, where he was one of the first to turn and run when the Jacobite clansmen charged. However, since it is thought that Duncan had no very strong loyalties to either side, but had been sent as a substitute for one of his feudal superiors, Fletcher of Crannach, we can have some sympathy for him. In later life he left Glen Orchy for Edinburgh and became an officer of the City Guard – effectively a policeman – before dying there in 1812.

Although Macintyre was illiterate, he was well aware of the works of other Gaelic poets, and friends transcribed his compositions for him. His own best poems are full of enthusiasm for the mountains, the deer, and the chase, but they were composed for singing or recitation, and do not fare well in translation. His long poem in praise of Beinn Dorain is generally considered to be his masterpiece, but a verse or two from his 'Final Farewell to the Bens' (*Cead Deireannach nam Beann*) demonstrate an enthusiasm which walkers on the Way will share:

> I was on Ben Dobhrain yesterday,
> no stranger in her bounds was I;
> I looked upon the glens
> and the bens that I had known so well;
> this was a happy picture –
> to be tramping on the hillsides,
> at the hour the sun was rising,
> and the deer would be a-bellowing.
> Blithely would I set out
> for stalking on the hill passes

Beinn Dorain from the south.

away to climb rough country,
and late would I be coming home;
the clean rain and the air
on the peaks of the high mountains,
helped me to grow, and gave me
robustness and vitality.
Farewell to the deer forests –
O! they are wondrous hill-country,
with green cress and spring water,
a noble, royal, pleasant drink;
to the moor plains which are well beloved,
and the pastures which are plentiful,
as these are parts of which I've taken leave,
my thousand blessings aye be theirs,

(from *The Songs of Duncan Ban Macintyre*, edited by Angus
MacLeod, Edinburgh 1952).

THE WEST HIGHLAND WAY

The Way crosses the Allt Chonoghlais at Auch by an old bridge of great character. Beinn Dorain looms steeply above, and a way can readily be found round the broken crags to its top. However, it may not be so easy to find a route downwards, particularly in mist, and Bridge of Orchy is probably a better starting-point for the ascent, since what that approach lacks in drama it makes up for in easier gradient.

Continuing on the old road, the West Highland Way turns left along the river flats and contours on a rising line across the foot of Beinn Dorain's great parabolic slope, beneath its runnels and gullies, to cross the railway, now returned from its long horseshoe bend to the east. This section of the Way gives pleasant, easy walking, looking down over the wide glen where the river winds gently north between alder-lined banks to join the Orchy, and forward to where Stob Ghabhar and its mountain peers in the Blackmount ranges begin to take their place as the next milestone.

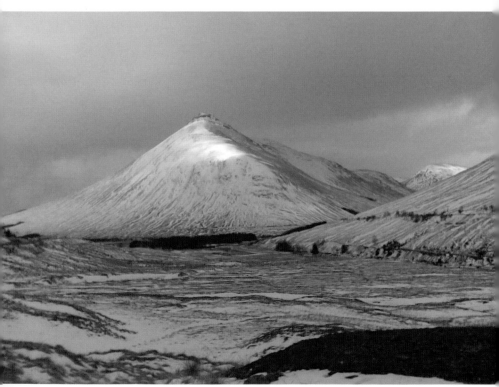

Beinn Dorain in winter.

Closer to Bridge of Orchy there are long views south-westwards down Glen Orchy, with, in certain lights, a singular feature in the long, upstanding quartzite dyke on the north spur of Beinn Udlaidh. Nearer at hand, the massive boulder of Clach a'Bhein may well have fallen from Beinn Dorain to come to rest amidst the moraine on the valley floor. Rightwards, the wild and rough Coire an Dothaidh divides Beinn Dorain from its sister peak of Dothaidh on the north.

Hereabouts the railway line runs down steady gradients towards Bridge of Orchy, before it begins its 37 km climb round the eastern edge of Rannoch Moor to its summit at 411 metres beyond Corrour Station. Thereby hangs a tale related by John Thomas in his history, *The West Highland Railway*, concerning the misadventures of a guard on the early morning freight train from Glasgow to Fort William. It seems the guard was sound asleep in his brake van at the rear when his driver's sharp opening of the throttle as the engine crossed the Corrour Summit broke the coupling of the van – which set off downhill, backwards, with its sleeping occupant. The signalmen along the line, loath to derail the runaway van with the guard aboard, let it run past at speeds of up to 55 kph. At last the van came to a halt on these rising grades south of Bridge of Orchy, where the stationmaster found the guard still fast asleep – and once more where he had been two hours before, having rolled back a distance of 40 km!

The Way enters Bridge of Orchy by the underpass at the station. The village, scattered along the axis of the old road between the station and the bridge, is one of those Highland settlements which appear on the map to be a major centre, but on closer acquaintance turn out to be just a few houses and a hotel. There are bus and train services north to Fort William and south to Glasgow. Anyone wanting to camp should ask at the hotel, as some of the land is owned by Forest Enterprise, who have a strict No Camping policy. Intending campers should note that the average annual rainfall recorded here between 1864 and 1873 was 3000 mm, and that similar levels can be expected from here on northwards, at least among the hills.

By dint of its strategic location on the southern fringes of Rannoch Moor, Bridge of Orchy has a role in two of the historical novels of Neil Munro, *John Splendid* and *The New Road*, in both of which the heroes make long and adventurous journeys northwards from Argyll into the central Highlands. In *John Splendid* the Bridge of Orchy itself is the scene for a missed rendezvous and a cryptic message. The hero's confederates had left on the parapet: 'three sprigs of gall, a leaf of ivy . . . and a bare twig of oak standing up at a slant . . . held down by a peeled willow withy, one end of which pointed in the direction of the glen'. These mystic symbols were interpreted to mean that three Campbells, a Stewart and a Gordon had gone hurrying south down Glen Orchy at 3pm the previous day! In *The New Road*, Aeneas Macmaster stops the night at the inn at Bridge of Orchy before crossing the Moor to Kingshouse by a devious mountain route to evade pursuit. The inn is described as: 'shabby to the point of scandal, no better than a common tavern, smoke-blackened, smelling of the reek of peat and mordants used in dyeing cloth; lit by cruisies, going like a fair with traffic', the traffic being mainly cattle drovers.

Both are excellent stories well told, but reflect more credit on Munro's lively imagination than on his historical research. The tale of *John Splendid* is woven into the history of the Marquis of Montrose's campaign against Argyll in 1645, about a century before there is any record of a bridge at Bridge of Orchy; and *The New Road* is set in about 1730, when there is no record of an inn, or indeed of any habitation at all, where Bridge of Orchy now stands. But these considerations should deter no-one from reading the novels, which not only evoke the landscape of the country around the Way, but also give a vivid sense of the tensions and insecurity of life in the Highlands of three centuries ago.

6
Bridge of Orchy – Kingshouse

SUMMARY

Distance: 19 km (12 miles).

Height range: 150-450 m. **Total ascent:** 350 m.

Accommodation: Hotels at Bridge of Orchy, Inveroran and Kingshouse. Bunkhouses at Bridge of Orchy and Kingshouse.

Supplies: There are no shops on this section.

Public transport: Bus and train services to Glasgow and Fort William from Bridge of Orchy. Bus services from the A82 near Kingshouse.

Terrain summary: From Bridge of Orchy to Victoria Bridge is straightforward, with one moderate climb. After Victoria Bridge the route follows the old road (good walking surface) across the western edge of Rannoch Moor, rising to 350m and very exposed in bad weather with no shelter of any kind until White Corries ski area is reached. Magnificent scenery, but in poor conditions a tough stage.

Rannoch Moor

It is impossible to set precise limits to Rannoch Moor, because a moor is as much a subjective experience as it is a geographical feature. But Rannoch Moor is usually taken as centring on the large triangular plateau bounded on the west by the Blackmount hills, on the south and east by Loch Tulla and the range from Beinn an Dothaidh to Beinn a'Chreachain, and on the north by the high ground from Beinn a'Chrulaiste to A'Chruach above Loch Laidon. The West Highland Way thus skirts only the western fringe of the Moor, but it does capture a good deal of the character of the place.

It may be debatable whether Rannoch is the biggest or bleakest of Scottish moors, but few would deny that it is the grandest. Its

Rannoch Moor.

fringing frieze of mountains, its irregular knolls and ridges, and its spidery tracery of lochs and rivers lend variety without diminishing its sternness. Geologically, the moor is described as a 'great granodiorite batholith', a relatively uniform mass of medium-grained grey granite, thought to be about 400 million years old. Its present form as a chaotically ill-drained, bog-blanketed basin results from its role as a major gathering-ground of ice during the last glaciation, combined with the effects of high rainfall and extreme exposure.

Despite its inhospitability and barrenness, Rannoch Moor has played its part in the human history of the Highlands. Its strategic location astride the main inland route northwards to Lochaber has led to a steady stream of traffic, military and civil, over the centuries: the old tag 'that thorofare of thieves' is only part of the picture. The story of the evolving lines of communication and their construction across the Moor is a romantic one in itself, while the hostelries on and around the Moor – Hobson's Choice for accommodation in an empty land – are well-known through travellers' tales.

The impression that the Moor creates will depend very much on the visitor's attitude and on the circumstances of weather and season: writers as various as Thomas Pennant and T.S. Eliot have been moved to record their reactions in prose and verse. In fine weather, with the lark overhead and the bog cotton snowy-white by tiny, calm pools that reflect the blue of the wide sky, the Moor belies its reputation as a desolate wilderness. In rain or snow with low cloud driving before a gale, it tends to promote the conviction that Hell need not be hot.

Bridge of Orchy - Inveroran
(4 km; 2.5 miles)

At Bridge of Orchy, the West Highland Way leaves the railway and the road which it has paralleled since Glen Falloch. It does not meet the railway again till Fort William, and the road not till Kingshouse, 18 km to the north. The first stage of the journey over Rannoch Moor is an introductory, short leg to the Inveroran Hotel by Loch Tulla.

The Way sets off westwards from the crossroads over the old bridge, beneath which the Orchy runs southwards over its bed of great rock slabs. The river must have represented a formidable obstacle to travellers before the bridge was built by the military in about 1751. According to General Roy's Military Survey, carried out at about the same time as Caulfeild's road-building programme in this area, the track over Rannoch Moor prior to the military road did not cross the Orchy at all; it ran north to Achallader, forded the Water of Tulla, and ascended the Blackmount on a line close to the present main road before striking westwards under Meall Beag to the route of the old Glen Coe road.

Just beyond the bridge, the Way leaves the old Glen Coe road, which holds to the flats along Loch Tulla side, and goes up through the forestry plantations on the military road, which here as elsewhere takes a direct route over the hill. This stretch over the Mam Carraigh was built around 1752-53, and has been less altered from its original state than most of the military road, for it seems to have been abandoned for the longer but lower route round the lochshore at an early date. When William and Dorothy Wordsworth came this way in 1803, it is clear from Dorothy's journal that they followed a road around the shore of Loch Tulla. The old road climbs gradually rightwards through the plantations, before traversing back and onwards again to a cairn at the highest point, 320 metres, on the ridge of Ben Inverveigh. In good weather this is one of the Way's most dramatic viewpoints. The whole range of the Blackmount Forest is spread out to the west and north, 'a wild tangle of long ridges and deep corries, with bold granite peaks and craggy outcrops', as W.H. Murray describes it.

To the north-east the broad sweep of Rannoch Moor leads round to the rampart of massive hills from Beinn a'Chreachain, by Achaladair and Dothaidh to Dorain, and then south to where the wide flats of Auch Gleann rise into the window of the pass through to Tyndrum. In the foreground below, Loch Tulla lies under the moor, with a dark scarf of woodland round its shores sheltering the Victorian lodge of Black Mount. The islet of Eilean Stalcair, with its few pines, appears to have been at least in part artificial, built up with timber and stone, though there are no evident signs of human habitation; it may have been simply a place of refuge.

Loch Tulla.

Under Mam Carraigh the magnificent pine woods that run down to the loch, the Doire Darach, represent another remnant of the ancient Caledonian pine forest. This particular wood has a special interest for ecologists, as the Marchioness of Breadalbane had some of it fenced over 100 years ago, to exclude deer and to encourage the regeneration of the pines. The whole wood conveys a sense of ecological vitality that is quite absent among the scattered pines of the upper part of Glen Falloch.

It is not generally realised that the Loch Tulla area has 'parallel roads' similar to the well-known features of Glen Roy, though these are less well defined. In certain conditions of light and vegetation growth, you may be able to trace as many as five terraces on the slopes either side of the valley of the Water of Tulla above Achallader farm. These ancient lake-shores were formed in the last glacial period when a lobe of ice from Rannoch Moor choked the drainage of the upper valley. As the ice gradually melted, it allowed the dammed-up waters to escape westwards by a succession of channels at progressively lower levels.

From its summit, the military road runs gently down towards Inveroran, giving a good forward prospect of the next section of the Way round the head of the loch and up onto the moor. The little hotel at Inveroran sits by the bridge on the Allt Grain. Facing east and sheltered by trees, it appears the very epitome of a snug haven in the wild country around. There has been an inn here for over two centuries; and standing as it does almost alone in the midst of an empty tract of mountain and moor, it has gathered its full share of historical and literary anecdote.

A little to the west, in a croft called Druimlaighart above the Allt Tolaghan, Duncan Ban Macintyre was born. For much of his life, he did not move far beyond Glen Orchy, and it is thus not surprising to find that he married the daughter of the Inveroran innkeeper, Mary, and immortalised her in another of his songs. The Wordsworths took breakfast at the inn during their tour of 1803, and though they were made very welcome, found the fare less than appetising: 'the butter not eatable, the barley-cakes fusty, the oat-bread so hard I could not chew it, and there were only four eggs in the house, which they had boiled hard as stones'. Nevertheless Dorothy observed with characteristic sympathy the scene in the kitchen, where:

. . . about seven or eight travellers, probably drovers, with as many dogs, were sitting in a complete circle round a large peat-fire in the middle of the floor, each with a mess of porridge, in a wooden vessel, upon his knee; a pot, suspended from one of the black beams, was boiling on the fire; two or three women pursuing their household business on the outside of the circle, children playing on the floor. There was nothing uncomfortable in this confusion: happy, busy, or vacant faces, all looked pleasant; and even the smoky air, being a sort of natural indoor atmosphere of Scotland, served only to give a softening, I may say harmony, to the whole.

Like the other old inns along the Way, at Inverarnan, Tyndrum and Kingshouse, Inveroran probably derived most of its trade from the droving traffic. There was a stance here, where the drovers could rest their beasts overnight and find grazing for them. In his classic account *The Drove Roads of Scotland*, A.R.B. Haldane tells us that something like 70,000 sheep and 840,000 cattle moved south by this route every year, and that the traditional grazing fees were 1/6d (7½p) for 20 cattle or 100 sheep. These facts emerged from a notable lawsuit brought by drovers against Lord Breadalbane, who in 1844 proposed to close the traditional stance in order to preserve his land for deer stalking. Breadalbane finally won the case on appeal to the House of Lords and the stance was removed to Bridge of Orchy. It is interesting to note that the drover named in the lawsuit as chief pursuer against the landowner was a MacGregor.

Inveroran also has an honoured place in the history of Scottish mountaineering, for the inn was the base of some of the earliest meets of the Scottish Mountaineering Club in the 1890s. The pioneers tackled some of their first winter routes in and around the icy Upper Couloir of Stob Ghabhar, the closest of the high Blackmount peaks. The Easter Meet of 1892 was also the occasion of a notable walking feat by two of the club's founders, W.W. Naismith and Gilbert Thomson. These two took a night train from Glasgow to Dalwhinnie, at the head of Strathspey, arriving at 3.30am. They walked down the shores of Loch Ericht, over the great plateau of Ben Alder, and across the full extent of Rannoch

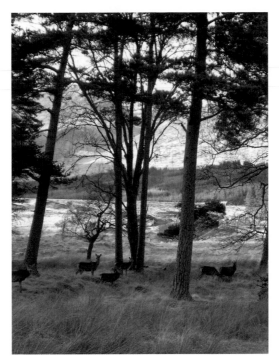

Deer among trees by Inveroran.

Moor, to join the Meet at Inveroran at 8pm. This jaunt of over 65 km, with a good deal of climbing thrown in, seems to have caused them no particular exertion, and both were out on the hills with their clubmates the next day.

The hotel now offers accommodation, meals and all modern comforts. Anyone wishing to camp should ask at the hotel. Tracks lead west towards the superb hills overlooking Glen Etive, with Ben Starav the prince among them, and a splendid low-level walk goes down Glen Kinglass to Taynuilt.

Inveroran – Kingshouse
(15.25 km; 9.5 miles)

From Inveroran the Way rounds the flats at the head of Loch Tulla, climbs on to the Blackmount, and skirts the western edge of Rannoch Moor under the flanks of the massive mountains that enclose Coire Ba. This stage has a natural unity: it was a day's journey for the old drovers, from one stance at Kingshouse to another at Inveroran. It is potentially the most serious stretch of the West Highland Way, for while there is an excellent track over the whole distance, it runs at a high level, is very exposed and virtually without any shelter for over 10 km, and offers no easy retreat in foul weather. In such conditions the choice is merely between pressing on and returning by the same route. It should be borne in mind that the western edge of the Moor has an average annual rainfall of 3,000 mm.

For the fit and experienced hillwalker, a superb alternative route is available outside the deer-stalking season (mid-August to late October). The high level traverse to Kingshouse over Stob Ghabhar and Clach Leathad is a classic ridge walk involving some 18 km of walking and around 1,400 metres of ascent, depending on the number of tops taken in. The SMC Guide *The Central Highlands* gives further details, and the route should definitely not be tackled without the appropriate skills and equipment; the route-finding is not altogether straightforward, and can be difficult in mist.

From Inveroran the Way starts gently, winding, first west, then north towards Victoria Bridge and Forest Lodge. In winter and early spring red deer can frequently be seen on the flats. Forest Lodge, set in a pine plantation, is a typical Victorian 'shooting box' with a hint of the Black Forest in its architecture, a product of the great deerstalking industry that dominated much of the Highlands in the late nineteenth and early twentieth centuries, reaching its zenith in the 30 or 40 years before the First World War. At that time the Blackmount forest was owned by the third Marquis of Breadalbane, whose favourite recreation was deer-stalking. His wife, too, was a keen stalker, and her account *The High Tops of Black Mount* is well worth reading. It is an unpretentious record of long hard days on the mountains in pursuit of the stag, and whatever your attitude to the hunt, the Marchioness's sheer enthusiasm for mountain and corrie, and her enormous relish of the physical toil and satisfaction of hill days, are irresistible. Appropriately, when the Ladies' Scottish Climbing Club was formed in 1908, the Marchioness became the club's first Honorary President.

The military road heads straight up the hill behind Forest Lodge, but the Way holds to the old Glen Coe road on a lower line, climbing gradually rightwards above the woods behind Black

Walkers on Ba Bridge.

Mount Lodge. The origin of the name 'Blackmount' for this area is uncertain, though it may well have referred to the peat hags on the moor. In the Highlands 'mount', or 'mounth', usually implies not a hill as such, but a high plateau, often with a pass across it. In this sense the title of Blackmount has been current since at least the late eighteenth century. The transference to include the deer forest and mountain range to the west seems to be more recent.

As the track climbs steadily towards its first summit on the moor, at around 320 metres, it gives a wide outlook over Loch Tulla to the Achaladair hills, but the focus of interest changes when the Way turns north. At the moorland summit between Meall Beag and Beinn Toaig you cross from Argyll and Bute into the Highland Council area for the remainder of the route; and from the Orchy drainage, flowing to the Atlantic, back into the Tay system. Attention now centres on the vast, wild recess of Coire Ba to the west of the road, and on the great mountains that form its walls and throw down craggy ridges to its wide, peat-hagged floor. It is not difficult to imagine glaciers pouring down from the corries under Stob Ghabhar and Clach Leathad to augment the huge ice field that once lay over the moor.

In summer even this wild scene has its charm. The drier knolls are clad in purple heather, the damp hollows in strong-scented myrtle; the wet flats are dotted with the snowy plumes of bog cotton and the golden-yellow spikes of bog asphodel, with the delicate pinkish-purple of the heath spotted orchid here and there. Wherever the underlying peat is exposed, bleached and gnarled remnants of pine roots may be seen within it. These former pinewoods, once extensive, may have suffered the same fate as other parts of the Old Wood of Caledon – reduction by cutting, burning, and grazing – but climatic factors may also have played a substantial part in their demise on this high, wet, exposed site.

Ba Bridge is perhaps the remotest part of the West Highland Way. The River Ba forces its way eastwards through a rocky gut and descends to wind across a wide boggy flat; to the west, rough ridges rise to high peaks. Coire Ba has always been a haunt of the red deer, and around the month of October, with the wind in the right quarter, you may hear the corrie resound to the calling of red deer stags in the rut. It is not a beautiful noise – a long, low, aggressive, throaty braying; but it has immense power to evoke the atmosphere of wild hills and open moor.

Coire Ba and its deer are the basis of a story dating back to the time of James VI and I. The King heard that a white hind, presumably a rare albino, had been sighted in Coire Ba, and despatched one of his servants, John Scandoner, to capture it alive. Unfortunately Scandoner arrived in the area in February 1622 and met the kind of weather that might be expected in Coire Ba at that season, He did sight the white hind, but despite the aid of a company of men lent by Sir Duncan Campbell of Glenorchy, he failed to catch it. Looking at the ground, it is easy to appreciate the difficulties he faced.

From Ba Bridge the Way climbs again, past the remains of Ba Cottage and the junction with a track leading down to the A82 road, which can be seen a few kilometres to the east, tracing a route between the large lochans on the flattest part of the moor. This summit is the highest point on the West Highland Way so far, at about 450 metres. Not far above this point, and visible from the southern approach, is a small memorial to Peter Fleming,

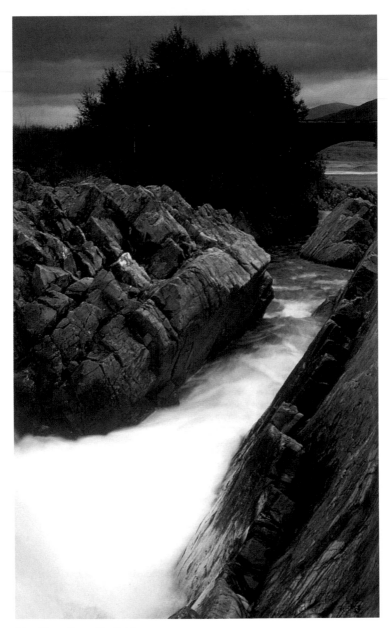

The River Ba at Ba Bridge.

who died of a heart attack while out shooting on 18 August 1971.
Fleming was a remarkable man whose career was full of incidents
no less colourful and dramatic than those inflicted on James Bond

Lochan na h-Achlaise, Rannoch Moor.

by his novelist brother, Ian Fleming. Among his travels, many of them as a special correspondent for *The Times*, he took part in an abortive expedition to the Amazon jungle in search of the long-lost Colonel Fawcett, and roamed widely through Central Asia. In World War Two, Fleming of necessity became a specialist in escaping from occupied countries, and he did so successively from Norway, Greece and Burma.

The memorial commands a superb panorama of the Moor, though the outlook might be characterised as 'Caledonia stern and wild', since it consists almost exclusively of mountain, moor and lochan, with not more than two or three human habitations in sight. Eastwards, the Moor stretches away in a patternless mosaic of lochans and pools, hummocks and boulders, boggy flats and bare hills.

From this bleak splendour the eye lifts to the encircling ranges. Many of the tops to the south will by this stage be old friends to walkers doing the whole Way, but you may be able to pick out one or two new peaks in Mamlorn and the Loch Rannoch area. Just to the south of the dip in the skyline through by Strath Tummel, Schiehallion may be visible as a slightly lopsided pyramid. The isolation and simple form of this mountain made it the subject of a four-month-long scientific programme in 1774, when the Astronomer Royal of the time, Nevil Maskelyne, used the peak to calculate the mass of the earth. To the north-east the huge plateau of Ben Alder may be seen, while the eastern tops of the Grey Corries range and the hills around Loch Treig appear over Black Corries Lodge to the north.

This extravaganza of mountain scenery continues as the Way follows the old road, here rather rough and broken in places, round the flanks of Meall a'Bhuiridh to descend gently into the wide basin that drains to the River Etive. Far ahead in the portals of Glen Coe you may spy the plantation at Altnafeadh, marking the foot of the Devil's Staircase track, by which the Way climbs over to Kinlochleven. To its left there gradually appears the dramatic and craggy bastion of Stob Dearg of Buachaille Etive Mor, 'the great herdsman of Etive', perhaps the finest of the Way's mountain mileposts. Like a neolithic arrowhead, in W.H. Murray's telling phrase, it dominates the whole of this part of the Way.

Under Meall a'Bhuiridh are the chairlift and other facilities of the Glencoe ski centre. The lift goes up to ski runs on the upper slopes beneath the summit of the mountain, above 750 metres. The skiing potential of Meall a'Bhuiridh was first explored by a party from the Ladies' Scottish Climbing Club as far back as 1917. In the mid 1950s a tow was set up and in 1960 the chairlift was built by Scotland's first commercial skifield company, White Corries Ltd. Skiing at Glencoe – as the area became popularly known – was never on the large scale of Cairngorm, Glen Shee or Aonach Mor (Nevis Range) beyond Fort William, partly because of the lack of nearby accommodation. However, it had a regular weekend clientele, particularly from the Glasgow area, and the runs on Meall a'Bhuiridh were renowned for their variety and quality. The area is now called Glencoe Mountain Resort and as well as skiing offers a wide variety of mountain biking trails, archery and other things. Facilities include a cafe and a number of 'microlodges', small wooden shelters accommodating up to 4 people each. Further details can be found at *www.glencoemountain.com*.

THE WEST HIGHLAND WAY

The Way joins the tarmac road up to the ski car park just opposite Blackrock Cottage, run by the LSCC and available to members
of kindred clubs. Blackrock is a small, snug hut of great charm,
with a unique and almost tangible atmosphere derived from its
lonely position. No-one who has the good fortune to stay there on
a clear autumn or winter night, when the silent moor and stark
peaks lie under a bowl of stars, will readily forget the experience.

From Blackrock the Way swings downhill over the moor,
crosses the main road which it last met at Bridge of Orchy, and descends towards Kingshouse Hotel, nestling among pines in a wide
hollow under the great, bare whaleback of Beinn a'Chrulaiste.
As the perspective changes on Buachaille Etive Mor, you will see
that Stob Dearg is not an individual rock peak, but the craggy
northern end of a range of ragged hills stretching down Glen
Etive. To complement it on the other side of the glen, the broken

Sron na Creise.

Walkers approaching Kingshouse.

ridge of Sron na Creise emerges from behind Creag Dhubh of Meall a'Bhuiridh. Kingshouse is thus framed in one of the noblest settings of mountain and moor that Scotland can show.

Kingshouse was evidently a going concern 200 years ago – not, perhaps, a long history by lowland standards, but remarkable for an inn in such a remote and uninhabited location. Indeed, the problems of running the inn were acknowledged by the Government, who for long contributed an annual grant to keep it open, and charged no rent. Nevertheless, the accounts of early tourists make it clear that the management of the inn left a great deal to be desired: in 1803 Dorothy Wordsworth, usually very tolerant of primitive accommodation, was forthright in her condemnation: 'Never did I see such a miserable, wretched place'.

The shortcomings in management may be explained by the concern of successive innkeepers with the business of salt-smuggling, a trade in which Kingshouse seems to have played an important part. Salt sounds an unlikely contraband, but at the end of the eighteenth century it was subject to a heavy duty – except where it was to be used to preserve fish for export: and that was the salt which was trafficked. Southey records that one innkeeper at Kingshouse made enough from salt in ten years to buy a farm and retire on the proceeds: 'the excise officers give very little interruption to this trade, because the value of a seizure is far from being an adequate compensation for the trouble and risque of making it'.

The hotel now boasts all the modern amenities including a bunkhouse. It is the only accommodation available, although more can be found in and around Glencoe village, some 19 km to the west, and the Glasgow to Fort William bus service on the A82 road provides a means of getting there.

7
Kingshouse – Kinlochleven

SUMMARY

Distance: 14.5 km (9 miles).

Height range: 250-550 m. **Total ascent:** 425 m.

Accommodation: Hotel and bunkhouse at Kingshouse. Hotels, B&Bs and bunkhouse in Kinlochleven.

Services: Reasonable range of shops in Kinlochleven.

Public transport: Regular bus services to Glasgow and Fort William from the A82 in Glencoe. Limited service to Fort William from Kinlochleven.

Terrain summary: From Kingshouse the Way enters the sublime scenery of Glencoe and at Altnafeadh climbs over the Devil's Staircase, an old military road, to its highest point at nearly 550m before a long descent into Kinlochleven. The route follows paths and good tracks but, although short, this is still a hard stage in bad weather. The compensation comes in glorious mountain views throughout.

The West Highland Way continues to follow the old military road as it runs westwards towards the head of Glen Coe, before climbing sharply northwards up the bounding wall of Rannoch Moor to the highest point on the Way, the top of the Devil's Staircase at 550 metres. From there the old road and the Way descend gently, contouring round the northern spurs of the Aonach Eagach ridge, until they make a final plunge to sea-level at Kinlochleven. In clear weather this stretch offers magnificent mountain views, first of the dramatic and rugged peaks around the head of Glen Coe and Glen Etive, and later of the great ranges between Loch Leven and Ben Nevis.

In bad weather it is potentially hazardous; there is no shelter at all on the exposed upper part of the Way between Altnafeadh and the buildings at the head of the Kinlochleven pipeline race

(GR 202604). While the Way is evident on the ground in fair weather, it would not be difficult to stray off it in mist or snow, with the possibility of wandering into some of the less hospitable parts of Rannoch Moor. On these hills, to sit down and wait for mist to clear is an invitation to exposure in any but the mildest weather: all walkers should have map and compass – and know how to use them.

Across the fine old bridge by Kingshouse Hotel the Way runs north to a T-junction where a signpost points boldly eastwards over the empty moor to 'Rannoch by Loch Laidon'. It is nearly 20 km under the slopes of A'Chruach to Rannoch Station on the West Highland Railway, where the public road from Loch Rannoch ends. The Way turns left and follows the old Glen Coe road west towards its junction with the A82. Directly ahead looms the pyramid of Buachaille Etive Mor, a great bastion between Glen Etive on the left and Glen Coe to the right. After almost a kilometre, when the concrete arch of the bridge on the main road is receding to the left, the old military road strikes off over a stile up the hill to the right. The old road begins as a rather faint track, but becomes more defined as it climbs on to the slopes of Beinn a'Chrulaiste. Its highest point offers a superb mountain panorama round from the bare moorland rising behind Kingshouse past

Kingshouse in winter.

The head of Glen Coe from Kinlochleven.

Meall a'Bhuiridh, Sron na Creise and Buachaille Etive Mor to the tops of the Three Sisters of Glen Coe. The route then ambles down as a pleasant heathery terrace to Altnafeadh, close to the main road for the last few hundred metres.

It is also possible to get to Altnafeadh by following a path beside the River Coupall. This alternative line continues on the Glen Coe road to the Glen Etive crossroads and along the main road for a short distance before it strikes across to the Coupall, following its banks up to the footbridge at Lagangarbh, below Altnafeadh. This route has a special attraction for those interested in geology, as it clearly shows a notable structural feature. The 'manie mightie steep hills upon Glen Koen', as Timothy Pont described them, are the product of a remarkable geological phenomenon, the cauldron-subsidence, of which this is the classic example, though similar features underlie Ben Nevis and the mountains round Loch Etive. In the Glen Coe case a ring-fault cut out a great block of lavas of the Lower Old Red Sandstone period, an oval about 14 km by 7 km. The block, in W. H. Murray's vivid image, 'foundered like a loose-fitting piston in a cylinder block of Dalradian schist', with molten magma rising around the edges of the sinking lavas to ring and fill the cauldron with granite. Subsequent erosion has carved the mountains out from the original lavas. At the eastern end of the glen, the precise line of the ring-fault is uncertain, but the margin of the granite is evident. In the bed of the Coupall as the river turns southwards in the wide waterslide down over the moor, banded grey Dalradian strata change over a short distance through a zone of contact into a strong red granite that forms massive slabs in the river-bed.

Both routes are dominated by the great crags of Buachaille Etive Mor, which make the mountain one of the finest and most popular rock-climbing peaks in Scotland. Some of the best-known features can be readily identified: the upstanding thumb of the Crowberry Tower below and to the east of the summit, with Crowberry Ridge falling from it; the bulbous bulwark of North Buttress, with steep walls and hard climbs on both its flanks: and the open chasm of Great Gully to its right, with the dark slit of Raven's Gully in its upper part, hard against the buttress. There are easier climbs, but they are not readily found by those unfamiliar with the mountain. For walkers, a relatively straightforward route goes up the corrie behind the SMC hut at Lagangarbh to its head in Coire na Tulaich, from which the ridge can be gained. Even so, this is a rough scree scramble at the top and demands an ice axe in winter or spring as well as careful compass work on the ridge in thick weather. From the top of this fine peak there is a wide vista over the Moor and north to the hump of Ben Nevis beyond the intervening ridges of the Mamores.

In common with most of Glen Coe, the Buachaille is owned and managed by the National Trust for Scotland. This property was the first of the Trust's Mountainous Properties, being purchased between 1935 and 1937 with funds contributed by members of the SMC, the Pilgrim Trust and the general public. Much of the money, as well as the initiative for the purchase, came from Percy Unna, then president of the SMC, who later be-

Buachaille Etive Mor.

queathed his substantial fortune to the Trust for similar purposes. The management of the Mountainous Properties is generally based on principles recommended by him; he felt strongly that the hills should be left in a 'primitive' condition, and should not be made easier or safer to climb. In this he showed remarkable foresight, long before pressures from recreation and tourism presented any real threat to such areas. Unna died in 1950, as the result of a heart attack on Beinn Eunaich near Loch Awe, on the eve of the Hogmanay meet of the SMC. He is buried in Pennyfuir Cemetery, just outside Oban.

From the main road by Altnafeadh, the Way strikes uphill by the burn, crosses it, and rejoins the old military road above the plantation. From here you can look south-west through the remarkable pass of the Lairig Gartain separating the two Buachailles, Mor and Beag. The distinctive shape and profound depth of the valley, with steep slopes swooping nearly 500 metres from the tops on either side, indicate that it has been much eroded by the Rannoch glaciers, but examination of the map will show an extra factor in its formation. It is possible to trace an almost exactly straight line from upper Loch Etive through the Lairig Gartain and Altnafeadh, across the Blackwater Reservoir and far to the north-east under Beinn a'Bhric and Beinn na Lap. This linear feature, a shatter-zone associated with a fault, has allowed the forces of erosion to work to greater effect, producing these sharply pronounced landforms.

The section of military road from Altnafeadh over to Kinlochleven has long been known as the Devil's Staircase, though that name is strictly applied only to the carefully engineered zigzags

The route north of the Devil's Staircase.

under the summit on the Rannoch side. From Major Caulfeild's report for 1750 it seems likely, though not absolutely certain, that the Devil's Staircase road was built during that year. Something like 450 officers and men were involved in the work. It seems probable that the troops themselves christened the zigzags the Devil's Staircase; Roy's map of 1755 has the name 'Mam Grianau' on the pass, but that name seems to have passed into obscurity.

The Roy map also clearly shows that there was a track of sorts down Glen Coe as well as over the ridge to Kinlochleven. As at the Mam Carraigh above Loch Tulla, the shorter, steeper route dictated by military priorities found little favour, and in 1785 the Staircase and the Lairig Mor road between Kinlochleven and Fort William were abandoned for an improved route by Glen Coe to Ballachulish and along the shore of Loch Linnhe. As a result, the wide and sinuous hairpins of the Staircase proper are reasonably well-preserved, with good kerbing and bottoming in parts. Erosion caused over the years by water, by walkers and by motorcycles (this is sometimes a stage in the Scottish Six Days Trial held in May each year) has been sensitively repaired.

There was no proper road here in February 1692, when the infamous Massacre of Glen Coe took place in the lower, inhabited part of the glen. Had there been a road, the Massacre might have been more brutal than it was, since it could have permitted the Government troops to complete their intended cordon of the glen to prevent the escape of the trapped MacDonalds.

The Massacre was the result of a complex interaction of political forces: between Hanoverians and Jacobites, between Lowlanders and Highlanders, and between rival Highland clans. Anyone interested in more detail will find full and readable accounts in John Buchan's *The Massacre of Glencoe* or John Prebble's *Glencoe*. In brief, the MacDonalds of Glen Coe fell foul of the Hanoverian strategy for the pacification of the Highlands, perhaps because they were a small clan with a reputation for reiving and raiding similar to that of the MacGregors. Through loyalty to the exiled King James VII, MacIain, the elderly chief of the clan, narrowly failed to take a prescribed oath of allegiance to William of Orange by the deadline set for the end of December 1691. Although more powerful chiefs had failed to take the oath altogether, the ambitious Secretary of State for Scotland, Sir John Dalrymple, decided

View from the Devil's Staircase.

to make an example of the MacDonalds. The king, embroiled in a full-scale war with France, gave his approval to measures 'to extirpate that sept of thieves'.

On 1 February 1692, 120 soldiers of Argyll's Regiment, commanded by Captain Robert Campbell of Glenlyon, were quartered on the people of Glen Coe. Although Glenlyon had suffered losses of property at the hands of MacIain and his men, he was also related to the chief by marriage, and the MacDonalds welcomed the troops into their homes without any suspicion of what was to come. On 12 February, the orders for the massacre reached Fort William from Edinburgh. Lieutenant-Colonel James Hamilton relayed the command to Campbell at Glen Coe through a detachment under Major Robert Duncanson at Ballachulish, and set off with 400 men to close the escape routes from the glen. Above the head of Loch Leven, however, Hamilton's force encountered a blizzard, and did not reach the upper end of Glen Coe until about 11am on the 13th.

By that time the grisly butchery of the Massacre was all but done. At 5am, in the winter dark, Glenlyon set his troops to fulfil the orders he had received, 'to putt all to the sword under seventy'. MacIain was roused from his bed and shot in the back; his wife was stripped, and her rings torn from her fingers. As the neighbours rose in alarm, they were murdered in their turn. In all about 40 adults were killed, the remainder fleeing to the hills under cover of the blizzard, in which an unknown number more died of exposure and starvation. The thatch of their houses was burned, the livestock driven off and Glen Coe left plundered and empty.

As the news of the Massacre became known throughout Scotland, public feeling rose against its perpetrators. At length, in 1695, a Commission of Inquiry investigated the outrage; as a result of its findings, Dalrymple lost his Secretaryship. Few others suffered any real retribution. But the memory of the Massacre and revulsion against it have persisted over three centuries: not so much for the scale of its brutality, since clan warfare had gener-ated many atrocities at least as bad, as for its appalling character – a ruthlessly calculated political mass-murder carried out by the trusted guests of the victims.

The last zigzag of the Staircase leads rightwards to the cairn on the summit. If you are favoured with clear weather, the view from this, the highest point of the West Highland Way, well repays the effort of getting here. Given time to spare, it is worth climbing the ridge westwards to the 707m summit of Stob Mhic Mhartuin for a wider prospect that takes in the rugged peaks on the south side of Glen Coe. For your own safety, however, you should not wander too far off the Way, as the ridge eventually leads to the narrow and difficult traverse of the Aonach Eagach. The new as-pect of this view is to the north, where the Way's final mountain milepost, the massive bulk of Ben Nevis, hunches against the crag of its great North-East Buttress. The shapely cone of Carn Mor Dearg provides a foil to Nevis on its right. Ranged in front, the Mamores present a surge of varied peaks and swinging ridges above the deep-cut Leven valley.

The old road pauses a little on the crest, then drops steadily into the rather boggy glen to the north, and contours along the spur on its western flank. Before long you catch your first glimpse of the Blackwater dam and reservoir to the north-east. These represent the power source for the aluminium smelter at Kinlochleven, and in a very real sense are the reason for the town's existence. The dam, nearly a kilometre long and over 25 metres high, was built between 1905 and 1909, and created a reservoir 13km long where there had previously been only three small lochs in a moorland valley.

Up to 3,000 men were employed in building the Blackwater scheme; it was one of the last great engineering projects built by navvies, the tough itinerant manual labourers whose muscle-power created the canals and railways of industrial Britain. Tales abound of the hard-working, hard-living, hard-drinking life of the Blackwater navvies; many of the stories can be found in the 'autobiographical novel' *Children of the Dead End* by Patrick MacGill, a remarkable self-educated writer and versifier. MacGill vividly describes the risks, squalor and lawlessness that were characteristic of life in the hills above Kinlochleven. He tells, for instance, of gangs of five men working ten-hour shifts on drilling – one man holding the steel drill between his knees while the others struck it with their sledgehammers in rotation: 'It is really a wonder that more accidents do not take place, especially since the labour is often performed after a heavy night's drinking or gambling. A holder is seldom wounded; when he is struck he dies.'

Materials and supplies were transported to the dam-site from Kinlochleven by an overhead rope railway known as the 'blondin' after the famous tightrope walker. It was a favourite ploy with the navvies to find spots where the buckets on the blondin could be reached from the ground with a long pole; then to identify and tip the buckets containing food or beer barrels, and scramble for the proceeds. It is also on record that a pedlar who was keen to trade with the navvies was maliciously induced to ride the blondin up to the dam at the end of a Saturday shift, and spent an unpleasant weekend in a stationary bucket high above the Leven gorge.

The navvies were of course a shifting population, and the movements of individuals – and in some cases, even their names – were unknown to their fellow-workers. During the five years of the construction work, a number of bodies were found in the area of the Devil's Staircase and in the wilds of Rannoch Moor: the remains of men who had set out for Blackwater and had been caught in bad weather, or who had made an expedition to

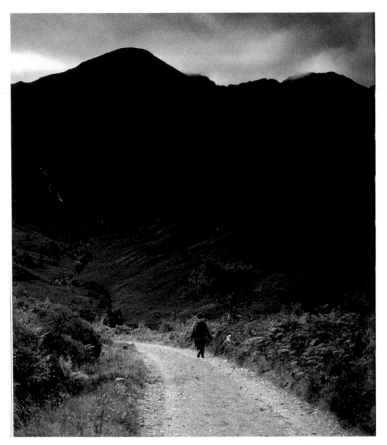

Approaching Kinlochleven.

Kingshouse for whisky and lost the path back in darkness, mist or snow.

As the Way rounds the end of the spur and descends to cross the Allt a'Choire Odhair-mhoir, more of the Blackwater works come into view: the culvert carrying the water along the valley flank to the penstock from which it rushes down six great pipes to Kinlochleven, and the access road and power line up to the dam. On the opposite side of the Leven glen you may be able to trace the feeder conduit to Blackwater from Loch Eilde Mor under the eastern tops of the Mamores, which was constructed during the 1914–18 War, largely by German prisoner-of-war labour. To the left, steep broken spurs fall northwards from the Aonach Eagach towards the abrupt and massive peak of Garbh Bheinn – well-

Kinlochleven factory site.

named 'the rough mountain' – which looms over Kinlochleven.

This is the country through which Robert Louis Stevenson made David Balfour and Alan Breck travel eastwards after the Appin Murder in *Kidnapped*. RLS clearly had a good eye for a rugged landscape setting. On the gradual descent towards the culvert and penstock you will notice the wealth of birchwood clothing the steep slopes of the craggy Leven valley and its tributary glens, a pleasing contrast to the virtually treeless moors you have crossed. These woods are partly the result of the roughness of the ground, which makes the young trees less accessible to sheep and deer; but they are also in part an unexpected by-product of the industrial development at Kinlochleven, since it provided an alternative employment for the crofters and shepherds of the area, thus reducing the level of sheep-grazing and allowing the trees to regenerate.

The crest of the spur on which the penstock stands is a dramatic viewpoint with a fine sense of height and depth. From here the pipes carrying the water from the dam plunge down 250 metres in a kilometre – the full head of water is about 300 metres – towards the factory site at Kinlochleven. Deep-set in the glen, a few houses at Kinlochmore appear in domestic contrast to the surrounding hills that rise 1,000 metres in steep broken slopes to rugged ridges. Although Loch Leven itself remains hidden among its flanking mountains, you can trace the line of the West Highland Way under the Mamore slopes and into the Lairigmor pass amidst the hills on the north side of the loch. Even in wild weather this is an atmospheric eyrie.

From the penstock the Way follows the works access road, winding steeply down into Coire Mhorair, crossing the stream beneath the little water-supply reservoir, and running down into the gorge of the Leven close above Kinlochleven. It parallels the pipes through the gorge and follows them down to the back of the former aluminium works, where it crosses them and turns right to a bridge over the river. Just upstream from the bridge an unmistakable red dyke of igneous rock crosses the river, catching the eye by its colourful contrast with the off-white quartzite on either side. The wall and abutments of the bridge repeat the theme in a chequerboard of red and white stone blocks.

Beyond the bridge, the Way turns left and follows Wade's Road – which ought by rights to be Caulfeild's Road – alongside a housing scheme as far as Morrison Crescent. It then turns left along a riverside path, into the centre of the town where it joins the B863 again by the bridge over the River Leven. Particularly after rain, it is worth taking the few minutes necessary to visit the waterfall on the Allt Coire na Ba: the path turns off Wade's Road just by the Episcopal Church.

Kinlochleven has a fair range of shops, cafes and a bank (the first since Drymen). There is also a choice of B&B accommodation, a hostel, a bunkhouse and a campsite. Kinlochleven is unique in the

Highlands as a 'factory town', and has had a curious evolution. In 1769, when Pennant breakfasted here 'on most excellent minced stag, the only form I thought that animal good in', there was only a tiny village on the flats at the head of the loch. By 1900 there were two small settlements, each with a deer-stalking lodge and a couple of cottages: Kinlochbeg on the south side of the river, Kinlochmore on the north.

Then came the aluminium works. Although it had originally been planned to build a factory and housing on the north side where more flat ground was available, difficulties with the land-owner and tenant of the Mamore estate caused the whole village to be built on the Kinlochbeg side under the lowering bulk of Garbh Bheinn, which kept the settlement entirely in shadow for more than two months in midwinter. Even so, the British Aluminium Company was required to build Mamore Lodge (now a hotel) high above the village to maintain the amenity of the Kinlochmore estate; and although small areas north of the river were feued to the Company in 1914, the problem of land for expansion went unsolved until 1935, when the Company bought the entire Mamore estate.

New difficulties arose as soon as the first houses went up at Kinlochmore, because the Leven formed the boundary between the counties of Argyll and Inverness. An inquiry in 1928 settled for the status quo, and until reorganisation in 1975 Kinlochleven had to contend with a series of minor problems and complex arrangements over local government, housing, education and medical services. There were even two police stations, one each side of the river, for a population of less than 2,000. Offenders in Kinlochbeg were taken to Oban for trial; in Kinlochmore, to Fort William.

Fifteen years after work had begun on the smelter and power scheme, Kinlochleven remained an extremely isolated place, with road access only by a rough cart-track along the north side of the loch, and a limited boat service. In 1922, however, the present road on the steep south flank of Loch Leven was opened, and in 1927 the north shore road was substantially improved. For nearly 50 years thereafter the Kinlochleven loop was a useful if circuitous bypass for the Ballachulish ferry at the foot of the loch, when summer tourist traffic congested the crossing, or after the ferry had

108

stopped for the night. However, the opening of the long-awaited Ballachulish bridge in 1975 removed the necessity to go round the loch, and Kinlochleven sees much less traffic now.

Recent years have thrust further change upon Kinlochleven. After a period of decline the smelter has now closed, and the town is being promoted and developed as a walking and climbing centre, for which it is well suited. Developments include The Ice Factor, a major indoor climbing centre housed in part of the former smelter complex. It is believed to be the world's largest indoor ice climbing facility, with nearly 500 tonnes of real snow and ice giving climbs of over 15m in height, suitable for all ages and abilities. There is also an aerial adventure course. The centre is open all year. For more detail go to *www.ice-factor.co.uk*.

8
Kinlochleven – Fort William

SUMMARY

Distance: 22.5 km (14 miles).

Height range: 50–335 m. **Total ascent:** 735 m.

Accommodation: Hotels, B&Bs and bunkhouse in Kinlochleven. Full range of accommodation in Fort William.

Supplies: Reasonable range of shops in Kinlochleven. Full range of shops in Fort William.

Public transport: Limited bus service to Fort William from Kinlochleven. Regular bus and train services to Glasgow from Fort William.

Terrain summary: The last stage of the Way involves a steady climb from Kinlochleven on a good track over the Lairigmor and another climb through forestry into Glen Nevis, both reaching a height of nearly 300 m, and the latter giving fine views of Ben Nevis and the surrounding hills. A final short road stretch leads into Fort William, the northern terminus of the route.

Lochaber

Like Lennox and Breadalbane, Lochaber is one of the ancient provinces of Scotland. Traditionally, Lochaber is considered to have included all the country north from Loch Leven to the Spean valley on the east side of the Great Glen, and the region between Loch Eil and Glen Garry, right to the west coast. For our purposes the West Highland Way enters the Lochaber area at Kinlochleven, and goes through a typical range of its scenery – high mountains dissected by deep valleys, bare upper glens and hill lochs, with sea-lochs reaching far into the interior – to the centre at Fort William.

The hub of the province also provided its name, for Lochaber is thought to mean simply 'the loch estuary', and thus to refer specifically to Inverlochy, near the modern town of Fort William.

Sunset over Lochaber.

This strategic centre controls a major crossroads where the Great Glen meets Loch Eil, giving access to the west, and the Spean valley, linking eastwards to Badenoch and Strathspey. Its military significance was acknowledged at least as early as the thirteenth century, by the building of Inverlochy Castle, later supplanted by successive garrisons at Fort William. From this central strong-point, Cromwellian and Hanoverian troops sought to control the powerful Jacobite clans of Lochaber, the Camerons and various septs of MacDonalds.

Evolving lines of communication also tended to focus on this area: the Caledonian Canal and the steamer routes in the nineteenth century; the military roads and their modern replacements; the West Highland railway and its spur lines to Mallaig and Fort Augustus. Fort William and its satellite towns on the Inverlochy flats have thus developed into one of the main commercial and industrial centres in the Highlands. Their combined population of over 13,000 is second only to Inverness.

Kinlochleven - Lundavra
(12 km; 7.5 miles)

The last leg of the West Highland Way from Kinlochleven to Fort William divides naturally into two almost equal parts, the break-point occurring at Blar a'Chaorainn, near

Lundavra, where the Way leaves the Caulfeild road to cross into Glen Nevis. The path from Kinlochleven to that point follows the military road the whole way, and generally gives excellent walking. It climbs sharply out of the Loch Leven valley to about 250 metres and rises gradually thereafter to the summit of the Lairigmor, 'the great pass', at a little over 330 metres. There is not much chance of going astray, but once again there is little shelter to be had on the higher part of this walk, and you need to be equipped to face all weather conditions.

The Way takes the B863 road as far as the north-western edge of Kinlochleven, branching off opposite the school to pass behind the filling station on the north side of the road. On this first stretch there are some clear remnants of the original road construction; the stone bottoming on the fords is particularly well preserved. The path climbs steadily through the birchwoods, with backward

The pap of Glen Coe.

glimpses of the loch below. Gradually Kinlochleven begins to recede into its cranny deep-set among the hills, and Loch Leven takes on its true fjord-like character. Westwards, the shapely cone of the Pap of Glencoe – Sgorr na Ciche in Gaelic – stands proud above the loch.

The path forks a short distance below the access road up to Mamore Lodge. The Way takes the left fork, crosses the road, and climbs steeply up by the old road beyond. After a few hundred metres, the path crosses a little woodland stream and rejoins the military road; from here to its junction with the Lairigmor track, it is excellently graded and drained. Although the climb is a steady one, there are good viewpoints that will offer a ready excuse for a rest. To the west the view down the loch is closed by the Pap and the rugged, knobbly spurs of Beinn a'Bheithir (Ben Vair) behind Ballachulish. To the south, broken and gully-scored slopes rise to the high, pinnacled crest of the Aonach Eagach, the north wall of Glen Coe. This aptly-named 'notched ridge' provides a superb airy traverse that can be thoroughly recommended to those with experience of mountain scrambling. Eastwards the line of the Way can be traced down round the spurs below the Devil's Staircase into the Leven glen, giving an encouraging sense of the distance that has been covered.

Once you have reached the Lairigmor track you have done most of the work, and the walking is easy, though the track does rise and fall a little. You are now, as Pennant put it, 'on the side of a hill, an aweful height above Loch-Leven'. However, once the last pines in the steep-sided gorge of the Allt Nathrach are left behind, the character of the route changes. The bare hill-slopes on either hand rise to enclose the glen and limit the view; the track pursues a rather lonely course onwards to the pass, with only a line of power poles for company.

The summit of the Lairigmor is an unspectacular flat col; since the glen turns north a few kilometres further west, there is no great revelation of a new landscape, but only a prospect of the wide glen stretching ahead. The Way descends gently past Tigh-na-sleubhaich, 'the house by the gullied slope', to the ruin of Lairigmor itself. From here, an old right of way path goes off left across the face of Mam na Gualainn and over the ridge to Callert on Loch Leven. This path connected the Lairigmor road to the Glen Coe road when there was a ferry across the loch to Invercoe.

The Way rounds the granite, gully-seamed spur of Meall a'Chaorainn and continues its gradual descent, but now to the north. In this part of the glen the crofters around Blarmachfoldach had their shielings, and traces of the simple stone huts can be found by the burns that cross the Way. The cattle would be brought up here to graze for eight weeks or so in high summer, and were usually tended by young folk, women and children, while the men worked the croft. Although conditions at the shielings must have been primitive, in general the Highlanders of old seem to have looked forward to the 'flitting' to the shieling as a holiday.

The glen is still grazed, though now mainly by sheep, and salt-licks at intervals by the side of the road are intended to supplement the meagre mineral content of the acidic soil in the area. There is a sheep-fank at the southern edge of the Forestry Commission plantation. Once the Way leaves this plantation, you will catch glimpses over to the left of Lochan Lunn Da Bhra, a pleasant little loch with a few pines around its shores. The name is somewhat obscure, but may be a corruption of a Gaelic compound meaning 'the castle in the water'.

The loch is supposed to have been the haunt of a 'waterbull', a malicious mythical beast which would emerge from the loch and drag other cattle in to drown. This is a variant on the Celtic tradition of the kelpie or water-horse, which lured young men to mount it – or, in some accounts, merely to stroke it. They were then unable to detach themselves from the beast, which would charge off into the loch with them. The mangled remains of the victim would reappear some time later.

At the information shelter at the northern end of the plantation, a short distance from the derelict house of Blar a'Chaorainn, the Way and the old military road, close companions since Glen Falloch, finally part company. The Way takes to the hill again as a last fling on its crossing into Glen Nevis. The military road, as a single-track tarmac road, rambles up and down past the crofts of Blarmachfoldach and Glengour before descending steeply down into the suburbs of Fort William above Ach'an Todhair (Achintore), and thence to the southern end of the High Street in the town (7.25 km; 4.5 miles).

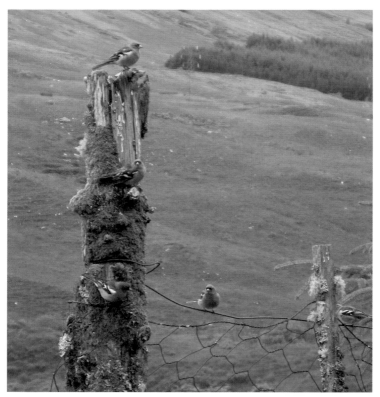

Chaffinches in the glen.

As a route this road is not without attractions of its own, including a wide prospect of the head of Loch Linnhe, with Fort William and its sprawling satellite settlements at Inverlochy, Caol and Corpach. It will have a particular appeal as an easier option for the weary or weather-beaten. Those favoured with fair weather, and still feeling fit, will prefer to take the more scenic and satisfying route through to Glen Nevis.

Lundavra - Fort William
(10.5 km; 6.5 miles)

The final stretch of the Way goes through the forestry plantations to the head of the valley behind Blarmachfoldach; a sharp descent into Glen Nevis is followed by a gentle concluding walk on forest tracks and public road to the centre of Fort William, where the Way ends. The crossing to Glen Nevis

115

offers excellent views of Ben Nevis at close quarters, and many who see the mountain from here in clear weather will be unable to resist the temptation to climb it as a grand finale to the Way.

The West Highland Way branches off the old military road just inside the forest gates at Blar a'Chaorainn, and climbs into a narrow break between the spruces. In places the path follows the old head-dyke, and accompanies it through the trees and over intervening stretches of open ground towards the head of the glen. This head-dyke marks the upper limit of improved ground around the settlements in the glen, separating it from the rough grazing on the mountain slopes. The dyke is at an unusually high altitude for this part of Scotland, partly because of topography and partly because of the underlying geology. The glen enjoys a southerly aspect, but is fairly sheltered from the prevailing south-westerly winds; and the rock formation beneath is the Ballachulish limestone, which helps to give a more fertile soil in a region where leaching by heavy rainfall tends to produce very acidic soils. In the eighteenth century there were three farming townships in the glen here, at Blarmachfoldach, Blar a'Chaorainn, and Tollie, with a combined population of perhaps 200. Today only a few crofts are worked at Blarmachfoldach; there are only ruins at Blar a'Chaorainn; and the remaining stones of Tollie, above the north bank of the Allt nan Gleannan, are vanishing beneath the Sitka spruce.

The Way enjoys an interlude of open ground, climbing over a viewpoint knoll above a former meltwater channel, before it goes back into the plantations, turning north-east towards the head of the glen. Beyond the rough slopes of Sgorr Chalum on the right, the mighty form of Ben Nevis, scarred by deep-cut gullies, begins to loom ahead. This is the south-western aspect of the mountain, the slopes that overlook Glen Nevis. The path to the summit follows roughly the left skyline from the col with Meall an t-Suidhe. Few would claim that the Ben looks shapely from this direction, but it impresses by its sheer bulk.

In the middle ground, the knobbly ridge-crest above Glen Nevis is of more immediate interest. The Way does not take the more obvious col under Sgorr Chalum; it descends a little to cross the long nameless burn running down off the spur of Mullach nan Coirean from the right, and contours roughly midway up the

Blar a'Chaorainn.

forested slope above the flats of the Allt nan Gleannan. It then breaks from the line of the dyke, and cuts left under the hill of Dun Deardail before climbing steeply up to the col north-west of the hill.

Dun Deardail is an Iron Age vitrified fort. Its elevated site has led to suggestions that it formed one of a chain of watchtowers from Oban to Strathpeffer, but it is difficult to trace any such chain, or to conceive of a plausible function for it. It seems more likely that the hilltop site was simply the best defensive position available in the area. The rubble walls of the Dun, now largely grassed over, were vitrified – fused into a glassy matrix – by fire. Vitrified forts are found so widely that it was for long felt that vitrification was a deliberate technique employed to strengthen the ramparts of the fort, but the many unburnt timbers which survive argue strongly against this. Archaeologists now assume

117

that the process occurred accidentally when the timber work lacing or fronting the masonry of the fort was burned by attackers. The etymology of the fort's name is doubtful; it does not appear on early maps. Some authors connect it with Deirdre, the legendary Celtic princess, but others translate it as 'the fort on the stormy hill', which has a more convincing ring to it.

At the top of the slope, the Way turns north over the col, with dramatic views of the Ben above, before dropping on to a forest road, turning left to begin a long, gradual descent into Glen Nevis. The harder walking is now behind you, and the view ahead, over the campsite and farmland of lower Glen Nevis, opens out to the wide lowland floor of the Great Glen around Inverlochy. Journey's end is in sight.

After 1.5 km or so, a branch road cuts back down to the right. The final spur off the West Highland Way, leading down to accommodation and service facilities in the glen, follows this road, turns down to the left, and crosses the flats to the public road by the River Nevis. Much of the valley floor is given over to a large caravan and camping site which in summer is a scene of colourful bustle and activity. A short distance up the glen, this branch of the Way ends at the Youth Hostel, a large wooden building by the road.

Glen Nevis itself merits a day or two for exploration. From various higher points in the glen, the Mamore tops appear to great advantage. It is ironic that from Kinlochleven on, the Way runs so close to them that their full height and shapeliness are not readily appreciated. Sgurr a'Mhaim and Stob Ban – the 'white peak' from its quartzite capping – form an effective backdrop to the lower part of the glen. However, the true glories of Glen Nevis are found in its mid-section, from Achriabhach to Steall, hard under the southern flank of Ben Nevis where mountain, river and woodland scenery blend in wild grandeur. Even in wet weather, that piece of country is an exhilarating experience.

The Way proper continues on the forest road through the plantation for another 600 metres or so, then turns sharp right and heads down to the public road in the glen, meeting it near a car-park and picnic site. On the left it passes close to a tree-covered knoll, the old cemetery of the sept of Clan Cameron who inhabited Glen Nevis. The Way follows the road above the river, passing a large erratic boulder known as Clach Comhairle, the 'stone of

The new ending of the West Highland Way at Gordon Square.

counsel', to which various stories are attached. The Victorian author of a local history took a sardonic view of one of these tales:

> The auld wives say that on a certain night of the year (the exact date they keep to themselves, for obvious reasons), the boulder turns round three times, and that anyone fortunate enough to find it on the move will get answers to any three questions he may put, before it finally settles to rest again. I am sorry I am unable to vouch for the truth of this legend from personal experience. Many a time and oft, by day and by night, have I passed this venerable relic, and have even had the reckless audacity to knock out my pipe ashes on its moss-covered surface; but it has never honoured me with so much as a tremor.

The route formerly ended at Bridge of Nevis. Now, however, the signs continue to Fort William's town centre and the new official end of the Way, at the 'Sore Feet' statue in Gordon Square. The lifesize statue of a walker sitting on a bench massaging his feet is by David Annand and was unveiled in September 2010. It provides a focus for the endpoint and gives a much better sense of arrival for those completing the walk. It also marks the start of the Great Glen Way which leads north from here to Inverness. Beside the statue is a carved Caithness stone map of the West Highland Way route. It is a good place for walkers to have their photos taken, and to sit and reflect on the walk they have just completed.

Fort William has a markedly diverse character; it is regional service centre, industrial town, and tourist resort. Virtually no trace remains of its main historic function, though its by-name in Gaelic is still *An Gearasdan* (the Garrison) and in English 'The Fort'. If you have time to spare, a visit to the West Highland Museum off the High Street can be recommended, both for its intrinsic interest and as further background to your walk on the West Highland Way. However, there is always the temptation of really rounding things off in style by climbing Britain's highest mountain . . .

Ben Nevis

The old pony track to the summit of Ben Nevis starts from Achintee, 2 km from Bridge of Nevis on the east side of the River Nevis; there are footbridges across the river from the car park opposite Achintee (where there is an information centre giving, among other things, details of the weather conditions at the summit), and from the Youth Hostel in the glen. Normal time for the ascent is about 3½ hours, and something over two hours for the descent, but the advice given by the minister of Kilmallie Parish in the *Old Statistical Account* remains sound: 'Few can perform a journey to the top of Benevis, and make proper observations, going and returning, in less than 7 hours; and still fewer, without feeling, in their limbs, the effects of the fatigue, for a day or two after.' (The record for the annual Ben Nevis Race, usually held on the first Saturday in September, is under 90 minutes up and down – a remarkable time by any standards.) When the minister was writing, in 1793, it was not yet certain that Nevis was the highest point in Britain. Ben MacDui, highest of the Cairngorm tops, was known to be of similar height, and the question was not resolved in Nevis' favour until the early nineteenth century.

Bear in mind that weather conditions on the summit are often dramatically different from those in the glen, and equip yourself accordingly. Many people have been caught out by being under-dressed for the higher slopes. The Achintee route climbs gently on the bouldery track from the old farm; the route from the Youth Hostel crosses the bridge opposite the hostel and climbs steeply to join the old pony-track. This has suffered from the passage of

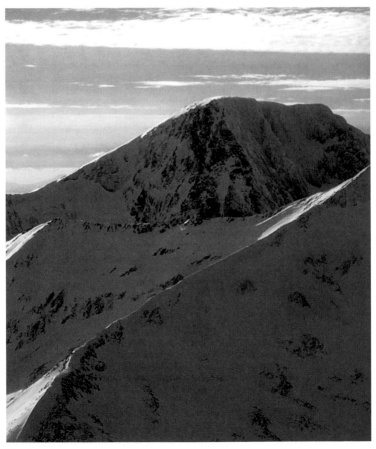

Ben Nevis in winter.

121

countless feet, particularly where descending walkers have cut the corners of the zigzags. To help minimise further erosion you should follow the path round and get the benefit of its easy gradients. The path was built at a total cost of £800, to serve the meteorological observatory which operated at the summit of the Ben from 1883 to 1904; at the turn of the century walkers were required to make a small contribution towards its maintenance. In recent years, large sums have been spent on repairing and restoring the path, and in some places it has been directed along an easier line.

The story of the Observatory is a truly remarkable one, well told in Kilgour's book *Twenty Years on Ben Nevis*. The meticulously detailed readings taken by the observers, often in horrendous weather conditions, are still being analysed today. The Observatory had to close due to a lack of funding, despite a public appeal. The summit path is but one legacy of its history.

The path leads round into the valley of the Red Burn and on to the col behind Meall an t-Suidhe. The upper part of the route zigzags up long boulder slopes, which can seem interminable unless compensation can be found in the ever-widening view or in observing the local geology. Nevis is another cauldron subsidence like Glen Coe, but a double one. The summit rocks consist of lavas representing the roof of a first, subterranean subsidence that collapsed into a second cauldron. The inner granite ring of the cauldron underlies the slope above Meall an t-Suidhe and is acknowledged by the predominance of Carn Dearg hill-names right round the Ben – Carn Dearg being 'the red cairn'.

The true character of Ben Nevis does not reveal itself until the summit is reached. From the edge of its broad plateau a confusion of steep rock ridges, buttresses, ribs and walls drop 600 metres north-eastwards to the Allt a'Mhuillin glen in one of Britain's greatest cliffs. In winter and spring, great cornices of snow and ice project over gully-heads and rock walls, and you should give them a wide berth. Scores of good climbing routes have been forced up these cliffs in a century of mountaineering in summer and winter; there is a special pleasure, your own toil accomplished, in watching the slow upwards progress of a roped party on ridge or buttress.

In good visibility the wider view from Ben Nevis is vast, though it inevitably has a somewhat flattened perspective, being above rather than among the surrounding hills. A small-scale map of

Scotland can be useful to identify more distant ranges. The summit of the Ben is now owned by the John Muir Trust and efforts are being made to reduce some of the summit 'clutter' such as various memorial cairns. There is continuing debate as to whether the final section to (and from) the summit should be waymarked to save walkers from straying close to, or even worse into, one of the deep gullies that bite into the summit plateau.

Once at the summit, Way-walkers can look southwards to where their route is marked by its mountain mileposts, and allow themselves a little well-deserved self-congratulation.

Appendix I
Gaelic Place Names

Gaelic place-names are found along the entire length of the West Highland Way, though in some places they have been corrupted and anglicised almost beyond recognition. In this guide the spelling used on the 1:50,000 Ordnance Survey map has been followed for the sake of consistency, though the map-makers themselves have not always achieved a successful resolution between local usage, anglicised forms and pure Gaelic. Thus the map has Achallader Farm under Beinn Achaladair; Beinglas Farm by the Ben Glas Burn; and Beinn Dubhchraig close by Ben Oss and Ben Lui. No attempt has been made to reproduce Gaelic accentuation in the guide.

Rather than give a long list of place-name meanings of which a good proportion will be doubtful in varying degrees, this appendix provides a short glossary of place-name elements, which should help you to decipher some of the commoner topographical names along the Way for yourself. The SMC District Guides include full glossaries of mountain names, and their excellent publication *Scottish Hill and Mountain Names* by Peter Drummond can be thoroughly recommended.

The definite article in Gaelic is highly variable according to the gender, form and case of the noun. In the nominative it may be *an, am* or *an t-* (masculine), *a', an,* or *an t-* (feminine) or *na, na h-* (plural). In the genitive—'of the'—it may be *a', an, an t-; na, na h-;* and *nan, nam,* respectively. Nouns also change in the genitive: thus *buirich,* 'roaring' or 'bellowing', but *Meall a'Bhuiridh,* 'hill of roaring'. And adjectives follow suit; *Coire Odhar Beag,* 'the small dun-coloured corrie', becomes *Sron a'Choire Odhair-bhig,* 'the spur of the small dun-coloured corrie'. The pronunciation changes too, but that is another story! Anglicised forms are shown in brackets.

ach, achadh (auch) field
allt burn, stream
aonach ridge or moor
ard, aird height, promontory

baile (bal- or *ball-)* hamlet, homestead
ban fair, white
beag (beg) little

bealach pass
beinn (ben) mountain
beithe birch
bidean pinnacle
binnean small peaked mountain
bo cow
breac (breck) speckled
buachaille herdsman
buidhe yellow
buirich roaring, bellowing

cailleach nun, old woman
caisteal castle
caol, caolas (kyle) narrow, strait, firth, kyle
caorann rowan tree
carn heap of stones, round rocky hill
carraig rock
ceann (kin) head, headland
clach stone
clachan hamlet
cnap hillock
coille wood, forest
coinneach moss
coire (corrie) a round hollow in the mountainside; cirque; sea-gulf, whirlpool
creag (craig) crag, rock, cliff
crom crooked
cruach heap, stack, bold hill
cuil nook, recess
cul back, hill-back

damh ox, stag
darach oak
dearg red
dobhran (dorain) otter

doire (derry) grove
druim (drum) the back, a ridge
dubh black
dun (dum) fortress, castle, heap, mound

each horse
eag notch
eas waterfall
eilean island
eun bird

fada long
fionn white, holy
fitheach raven
fuar cold
fuaran well, spring

gabhar goat
garbh rough
geal white
giubhas fir
glas grey, green
gleann narrow valley, glen
gorm green, blue
guala, gualainn shoulder of a hill

inbhir (inver) confluence
inis (1) island; (2) meadow by river; (3) resting place for cattle
iolair eagle
iubhair yew

lagan little hollow
lairig a pass
laoigh (lui) calf
leac (leck) flat stone, slab

leacach stony slope
leathad slope, brae
leitir (letter) slope, side of a hill
loch, lochan lake; small lake

mam large, round or gently
   rising hill; pass
maol bare top
mheadhoin (vane) middle
meall a round hill
mor large, great
muileann mill
mullach top, summit

nead (nid) nest

odhar (our) dun-coloured

righ king
ros promontory, wood

ruadh red, brown
ruighe slope, run for cattle,
   shieling

sgorr, sgurr rocky peak
sron nose, point, spur
stob point
stuc peak
suidhe seat; level shelf on
   hillside

tairbeart (tarbet) portage,
   isthmus
tigh house
tulach knoll, hillock

uisge water, river

Appendix II
OTHER LONG-DISTANCE
ROUTES IN SCOTLAND

Readers may be interested in other opportunities for long-distance walking and cycling in Scotland. A network is steadily growing through development by Scottish Natural Heritage, local authorities, tourist boards and partnership groups. Some of the routes currently open are listed below.

The **Southern Upland Way** crosses southern Scotland from coast to coast, running from Portpatrick, near Stranraer, east to Cockburnspath in Berwickshire, a distance of 340 km/212 miles. The route is waymarked with the same symbol of a thistle inside a hexagon as the West Highland Way, and its maintenance is similarly supported by SNH.

The official route guide, with special maps, is published by Mercat Press/Birlinn. Other guides are published by Constable

Loch Trool on the Southern Upland Way.

and Aurum Press. A free trail leaflet and accommodation and facilities guide can be obtained from Countryside Ranger Service, Scottish Borders Council, Harestanes Visitor Centre, Ancrum, Jedburgh, TD8 6UQ (tel/fax 01835 830281). Route details from *www.dumgal.gov.uk/southernuplandway*.

The SUW passes through a great variety of scenery and reaches its high point at over 700 m on Lowther Hill above Wanlockhead. It is a demanding and strenuous route, crossing the grain of the land for much of the way. Highlights include Glen Trool, Wanlockhead (Scotland's highest village), St Mary's Loch and the ancient track over Minch Moor past the tall Three Brethren cairns.

The **Speyside Way** runs for 105 km/66 miles from Buckie to Aviemore. It too is waymarked with the thistle inside a hexagon. There is a guidebook published by Rucksack Readers; route leaflets can be obtained from Moray Council Ranger Service, Boat of Fiddich, Craigellachie, Aberlour AB38 9RQ (tel: 01340 881266) and there is a Harvey strip-map of the route. The route's website is at *www.speysideway.org* (e-mail: *speyside.way@moray.gov.uk*)

The Speyside Way starts at Buckie on the Morayshire coast and runs west to Spey Bay. It then largely follows the River Spey upriver to Aviemore. Part of the route is on an old railway line. Highlights include Telford's superb bridge at Craigellachie, several distilleries which can be visited, and the views to the Cairngorm hills. Preparatory work is under way with a view to extending the route south to Newtonmore.

The **Great Glen Way**, which opened in 2002, starts in Fort William at the point where the West Highland Way ends and runs up the Great Glen through Fort Augustus, past Loch Ness (will you see Nessie?) to Scotland's Highland capital, Inverness, on the Moray Firth. The route is some 118 km (73 miles) long. It is a relatively low-level route using the Caledonian Canal towpath, forest tracks and roads, part of the old railway line from Fort William to Fort Augustus and a drove road. Contact the Great Glen Way Rangers on 01320 366633, *greatglenway@highland.gov. uk*, *www.greatglenway.com*. There is a Rucksack Readers guide and a Harveys map of the route.

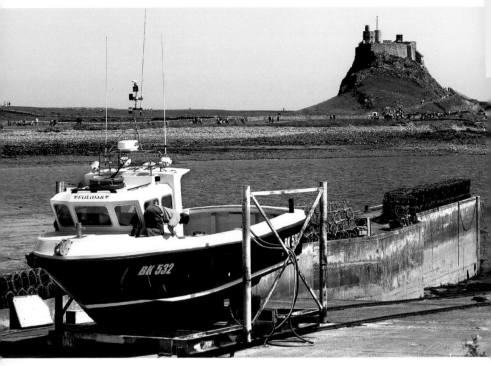

Lindisfarne at the end of St Cuthbert's Way.

St Cuthbert's Way opened in 1996. It runs from Melrose, in the Scottish Borders, to Holy Island, off the Northumberland coast, linking places associated with the life of the 7th century bishop, St Cuthbert. The route is 100 km/62 miles long, and is waymarked with the symbol of St Cuthbert's Cross.

The official trail guide, fully illustrated and with maps of the entire route, is published by Mercat Press/Birlinn. The route map is available separately, printed on waterproof paper. A trail leaflet is available free from VisitScotland, Shepherd's Mill, Whinfield Road, Selkirk, TD7 5DT (tel 0870 608 0404, e-mail: *info@scot-borders.co.uk*). Route details can be found on *www.scot-borders.co.uk* or *www.stcuthbertsway.fsnet.co.uk*.

A true cross-Border trail, this walk joins together a number of places linked with St Cuthbert, who started his ministry at Melrose in the mid-seventh century AD and ended it at Lindisfarne, the Holy Island off the Northumberland coast. The walk starts at the superb ruin of Melrose Abbey and climbs to cross the Eildon

Hills, before joining the River Tweed. Other highlights include the Roman Road Dere Street, the Cheviot foothills, St Cuthbert's Cave and the crossing of the sands to Lindisfarne.

The **Fife Coastal Path**, linking the four great bridges crossing the Forth and Tay at Queensferry and Dundee, was completed during 2003. There is no full guidebook. Leaflets covering the different sections are available from Tourist Information Centre, 19 Whytescauseway, Kirkcaldy KY1 1XF (tel 01592 267775). Route details from the trail website on *www.fifecoastalpath.co.uk*. A general guide to the Fife Coast, *Along the Fife Coastal Path*, which covers the route well with maps of the Path as well as pictures, is written by Hamish Brown and published by Mercat Press/Birlinn.

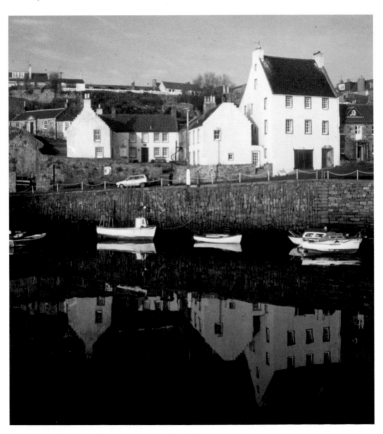

Crail harbour on the Fife Coastal Path.

The Fife Coastal Path provides a walk of considerable attraction and variety, with excellent birdlife and a large number of historic sites, museums and interesting towns and villages. The route has particularly good public transport links by bus and train, making linear walks along sections of it easy to arrange.

The **Ayrshire Coastal Path** runs for 161 km (100 miles) from Glenapp in the south to the county boundary near Wemyss Bay in the north. It was developed by local Rotary Clubs and is fully waymarked. The Rotary Clubs have published an excellent guide-book to the route. The walk passes through Girvan, Ayr, Troon, Largs and other coastal towns and villages. There is a website at *www.ayrshirecoastalpath.org*.

The **Borders Abbeys Way** is a circular route linking the four great Border Abbeys of Melrose, Dryburgh, Jedburgh and Kelso and also taking in Hawick. It is 109 km (68 miles) in length and offers generally easy walking. There is a website at *www.scotborders. gov.uk/bordersabbeysway*. A separate but linked cycleroute has also been developed,

The **Cateran Trail** is a circular route in Highland Perthshire through very attractive scenery and including Blairgowrie (the usual starting point), Bridge of Cally, Kirkmichael, Spittal of Glenshee, Glen Isla and Alyth. It takes its name from the caterans or cattle rustlers of former times who knew the hill tracks and passes covered by the route intimately. There is a website at *www. caterantrail.org*.

The **Kintyre Way** starts at Tarbet and runs south down the beautiful Kintyre peninsula to the village of Southend, a distance of 140 km (87 miles). Along the way it criss-crosses the peninsula several times and passes through a number of attractive villages, and you have the opportunity to visit the Mull of Kintyre with its lighthouse, made famous by Paul McCartney's song. There is a trail website at *www.kintyreway.com*.

The **Formartine and Buchan Way** is a footpath and cycleway following disused railway lines in Aberdeenshire from Dyce

Station, north of Aberdeen, to twin northern termini at Fraser-burgh and Peterhead, a distance of about 65 km/40 miles. There is no full guidebook, but route leaflets are available from VisitScotland, 27 Albyn Place, Aberdeen AB10 1YL (01224 632727), and there is a trail website: *www.buchan.org.uk/stricfbw.htm*.

A total of 22 walking and/or cycling routes plus one canoe route (through the Great Glen) are jointly promoted as Scotland's Great Trails. An illustrated leaflet is available from Tourist Information Centres or via *visitscotland.com/surprisetrails*. There are also a number of routes such as the East Highland Way and the Cape Wrath Trail which are not waymarked on the ground but are only described in guidebooks.

Index

OFFICIAL WHW MERCHANDISE

Why not treat yourself to a commemorative tee-shirt or official certificate of completion to celebrate completing the West Highland Way. This exclusive range of official West Highland Way merchandise has a choice of gifts for everyone.

It's easy to buy online from our shop
www.whwshop.com
We accept Paypal and items are despatched within 7 days on receipt of your order.

CERTIFICATE OF COMPLETION

OFFICIAL PASSPORT

THE OFFICIAL WEST HIGHLAND WAY

PASSPORT

KEYRING

PENS

WHW TARTAN SCARF 100% LAMBSWOOL

WHW TARTAN TIE

CAR STICKER
SCOTLAND'S PREMIER LONG DISTANCE ROUTE
WWW.WEST-HIGHLAND-WAY.CO.UK

TEE-SHIRTS

WHW MOUSE MAT

PIN BADGE

By purchasing official merchandise you are contributing towards the upkeep and maintenance of the West Highland Way.   *Thank you!*

www.whwshop.com